T0368534

Flurries

by
D.G. Mago

authorHOUSE®

AuthorHouse™
1663 Liberty Drive
Bloomington, IN 47403
www.authorhouse.com
Phone: 1-800-839-8640

Published by AuthorHouse 10/10/2014

ISBN: 978-1-4969-4150-3 (sc)
ISBN: 978-1-4969-4149-7 (e)

Library of Congress Control Number: 2014917162

Dedication

This book is dedicated to my Mom and Dad. Thanks for raising me the right way: with love, attention, patience and empathy. Thanks for giving me a sense of individuality, independent thought, and the room to grow into adulthood without the shadows of abuse or neglect. Every parent should use you as their model! Sadly, my father passed away from pancreatic cancer before this book was published. However, he did read the rough draft and saw the dedication, which was extremely important to me; he was always my biggest supporter. I hope you can find peace, Dad, so you may finally rest easy.

As in my first novel, Shelterball, the chapters are divided not by numbers, but by song titles. I wrote this book like it was a movie that I pictured in my mind. Therefore, it is the soundtrack for the book so to speak. All of the poetry in the book is completely original and done solely by me, the author, D.G. Mago. Artwork provided in the book has been beautifully and professionally done by two fabulous artists: stained glass artist Kathleen Goldstein for her paintings (**Chicki** and **Escape**, the latter being the background for the cover) and pop surrealist artist Heidi Hayes for her sketches (**Grenade, Fish, Magic** and **Hot Seat**) and her paintings (**Waiting** and **Unveiling of a Magician's Umbilical Cord**). Thank you both so much for your contributions to Flurries! All materials have been copyrighted. No images or content of this book may be copied or reproduced without written consent by the artists and author. DG Mago can be reached at <u>diacachimba45@gmail.com</u> for any questions or comments.

LL Cool J- "Rock the Bells"

Tick, tick, tick, tick…. The clock on the wall reads 2:59 pm, even though it is not a digital clock. It is an ancient, generic public school clock that can barely hold onto the wall. As Diego watches the red second hand drift slowly, his breathing becomes slower and deeper. Inhaling and exhaling have suddenly become very apparent. Moving clockwise towards the dreaded number twelve, the second hand creeps its way northbound. All the while, his eyes dilate, and his heartbeat increases. It is excruciating to watch it move in slow motion, like a tiny sailboat seen miles away from the shore. Sweat accumulates on his forehead and his feet begin oscillating uncontrollably under his desk; he dabs his forehead with the sleeve of his shirt back and forth. Ordinarily, 3:00 pm would be received with cheers and jubilation, but not today. Because this day at 3:00 pm does not represent freedom; on the contrary, today it signifies a challenge to his manhood or more accurately his adolescence.

Earlier in the day, a petition was being passed around the hallways about the U.S. government intervention in the Middle East, and Diego had it in his possession. The class bully, named Davis, snatched it from his hands and Diego objected. Reacting solely from reflex, he swung the back of his hand in protest attempting to get the boy's attention and tap him in the chest. However, the boy moved suddenly and he received the back of Diego's hand right in his eye. Diego was shocked, not only that he retaliated against the much bigger rival, but that he actually seemed to make the gargantuan flinch. The look on Davis' face was classic and he wished he kept a picture of it.

<u>Davis</u>-*If I have a black eye later, you're dead after school!* Diego knew he didn't hit him hard enough to do any damage so he resumed his normal routine in school. Much later in the day, Davis and three of his boys surprised Diego and threw him up against a locker. He pointed to his eye which had swollen up and closed halfway as he twisted the front of Diego's new dress shirt. The shirt is not actually new, just new to him. It, like most of his other clothes, is a hand-me-down.

<u>Davis</u>-*3:00, you're dead meat!* He said it in such a way as to force Diego's heart to pump twice as fast as usual, like a hummingbird floating in mid air, searching for a quiet place to quench its thirst. Ever since that moment, he has been unable to concentrate on anything else all day. Not only does he have to worry about Davis, but he had his boys with him; so even if he is lucky enough to get a quick victory, it

will be short lived. Davis is about eight inches taller than Diego and weighs a good 40 pounds more. He has an afro, but the guys always make fun of him behind his back, way behind his back, that he has a napfro, because his hair is often nappy (not brushed). Never would this be told to his face, only by Gabe who is afraid of nobody. More than a few times, Gabe has said that Davis looks like a big bear with a rotten tooth dangling from the top row of his mouth.

Diego is 13 years old and lives with his grandparents. Both his mother and father have passed away; they were both intravenous drug users and died of the HIV virus. He was told of their passing, the day before he turned 8 years old. He was devastated by their death and was never the same. It took him almost two entire years to come out of the funk he was in. Depression consumed him and his grandparents were very patient with him. Now, he is just as close to his grandparents as he was to his mother and father. In actuality, he now views them as his parents and worries about them all the time. His grandparents are old school; they came to New York from Puerto Rico as teenagers during the period where New York was importing cheap labor. They are honest people and are very religious. Diego has a crew cut, hazel eyes, and has just started to break out in pimples on his forehead. Confronted with puberty, his voice often wavers at the most inopportune moments, causing him even further mortification. He likes his fingernails cut and doesn't like the feel of it when they have more than a week growth. His distaste for little forks always makes him say he is boycotting them. He only uses big forks; the concept and practical uses of salad forks make no sense to him at all.

As the red hand is now only inches away, and approaches the twelve, the saliva in his mouth intensifies and he gulps. **Ring!** The bell sounds and pandemonium begins. All the kids scamper out into the hallway immediately closing off their auditory powers to the last minute instructions of the teachers. Diego, however, does not join in the party; he sits for a moment contemplating his course of action. His teacher looks at Diego with a disconcerted look as one of his eyebrows raise; he wonders to himself why Diego has not joined in with the bedlam that has initiated in the hallway. Of course Diego is scared; he is rather small for his age. However, he is from the projects and has grown up accustomed to fighting, although he does not enjoy it in the least. Slowly and reluctantly, he gets out of his chair, which is attached to the desk. As he gets up, he bangs into the corner of the desk, moving the one piece unit out of place. It screeches as it drags across the floor and it startles him. He puts his things in his torn book bag, and exits with caution out into the hallway. As he looks down the left side of the hallway, then the right side, the coast seems clear, but only for the moment.

It is no secret that there is going to be a fight today; word about things like this spread like a wildfire in northern California on a hot, dry day. Waiting by his locker is his best friend Gabe, who contrary to Diego is rather large for his age. Gabe is 14 years old and lives in the same building as Diego. He lives with his father and two sisters; his mother is addicted to crack and nobody knows her whereabouts. She has been missing in action for almost two years now. She had been a weak individual, always was. She had an alcoholic father and was taught to deal with her problems by using drugs or alcohol. She had no positive role models and when there were problems with the family, financially and emotionally, she did what she knew. When Gabe thinks about her, he quickly moves on, because he doesn't even want to wonder the unimaginable things she may have done on the street to get some money just to survive. Gabe has curly dark brown hair and already has hair on his upper lip; he is trying to make himself look older deliberately. He shaves it every few days, trying to get it thicker. He has a lanky build, but has broad shoulders and a small waist which could make him seem muscular. His voice is already matured; it is deep and smooth. Something about it automatically commands respect from others, even adults. He has dark eyes which are endless like a long lost mystical cavern. Some odd tidbits about him that nobody knows are that he likes the smell of paprika and also the way the word sounds. He dislikes the mesh in a bathing suit lining and will rip it out the first chance he gets. Unlike Diego, Gabe likes to fight and tells his buddy that if there is more than one boy there, he will jump in and help. He also stated he would be glad to be Davis' dentist this afternoon, and knock that rotten tooth out with a good uppercut. Diego laughs briefly before he recognizes the seriousness of the situation.

Diego-*No, this is my fight… I think I can take him.* He tries to convince himself over and over. What he momentarily forgets about are the other boys that may jump in.

Gabe-*Just crack him right in that snaggletooth!!* He demonstrates swinging his arm directly upward. *Even the tooth fairy wouldn't want that one!* Diego is too consumed with anxiety to laugh at Gabe's attempt to bring levity to the situation.

As they walk towards the exit, the muffled sounds of *fight, fight, fight,* become more audible from beyond the corridor. Already there is a crowd outside waiting to witness the bout which is getting larger by the minute. Most are there to see a beating; in actuality, they want to see blood like a couple of gladiators in the arena. Gabe walks slightly in front of Diego, hoping he can get his hands dirty today. The shouts become louder and louder. As they get closer to the crowd, Gabe changes the subject and tries to get his friend in a better frame of mind. He slows his pace and faces Diego, who has to look up to make eye contact.

Gabe-*Man you missed it. Today in teen living* (a class that used to known as home economics class), *we were making pizza, and when Cruz's group wasn't looking, I shredded some Ivory soap on their pizza, and it looked so much like cheese, they didn't even notice.* He starts to laugh out loud as Diego laughs heedlessly, even though he is in his own world right now. He begins pondering his boxing tactics in his mind.

Diego-*I'm gonna punch him in the stomach first, then in the mouth, in that rotten ass tooth, before he has a chance to hit me…before he even knows it's coming…*His eyes bulge out of his head and even though it is winter, sweat is falling from beneath his baseball hat and down the sides of his face. A few people chant Diego's name as he puts down his tattered book bag and scans the crowd. *No way! He didn't show!* Diego thinks perhaps he is waiting to make an entrance like James Brown so he waits. As the crowd gets antsy, people begin to disperse. With his anxiety level at an all time high, Diego sure is hoping that he doesn't show. He scans the crowd making sure they don't jump out of the crowd and attempt to bum rush him. Gabe cracks his neck and rolls his head around his shoulders a couple times.

Gabe-*Shit, looks like he was scared. Good thing for him anyway, that snaggletooth was coming out, son, he was gonna get roughed up good, wasn't he?* He waits for a response while he cracks his knuckles one at a time. Diego nods his head in agreement but is thinking something totally different. He truly didn't want to fight today. He remembers his mother and father fighting all the time, verbally and physically, and he would always get nauseous and throw up. Often, when he was smaller, he would hide under his bed in the fetal position, cover his ears, and hum to himself to drown out the verbal tidal wave that would engulf everything in the apartment. The uneasy feeling in his stomach right now is difficult to control; however, he manages to keep the pizza bagel, butter crunch cookies and chocolate milk that he had for lunch down for the time being. Now he has to talk a big game since Davis is nowhere to be found.

Diego-*I was gonna teach that boy a lesson!* His breathing finally returns to normal. *Dam snaggletooth!* Now that it appears obvious that indeed he was stood up, he boasts and brags a little bit. His anxiety falls like a punch-drunk boxer to the canvas. He double-checks and makes a complete 360 degree turn, making sure he sees no signs of Davis.

Descarga Boricua - "Fuerza Gigante"

As the crowd dwindles down to only a few, the two boys are approached by the rest of their crew. Robert Cruz, who they just call Cruz, lives in the building adjacent to them with his older sister as his caretaker. His father was deported to Mexico two years ago. He was an honest man who just wanted to support his family; he worked hard and was a very honorable man. Once he got deported, his mother could not deal with being alone, without a man. Shortly thereafter, his mother hooked up with another man and moved him into their home. When that was a total disaster, she simply left and never returned. Unprepared and overwhelmed, his sister stepped up and found some strength she didn't even know she had. She assumed guardianship of her brother and should be commended for the job she has done with very little assistance. She is very independent and uncompromising. Her relationship with Cruz has gotten stronger through this ordeal. He is 14 years old with black wavy hair. He has a medium build, dark brown eyes, and has a scar on his arm from where his mother's boyfriend stabbed him when he was drunk. Even though he received 34 stitches, somehow he managed to take that same knife and stab the boyfriend in the thigh; he still has nightmares about that night, although he will never admit it, not even to himself. As a result, he would sporadically sleepwalk, which he hasn't done in quite some time. He likes to fold old and used napkins and paper towels and store them away in a drawer in the kitchen. He dislikes the singer Jose Feliciano, and for some bizarre reason, whenever he hears a song sung by that singer, he begins to projectile vomit. He tries to improve his vocabulary each and every day. Today in school, he learned some words in Korean, which he found simply fascinating. While he talks, he folds his array of disorganized papers together and puts them in his book bag.

Cruz-*He's all talk anyways. That's all he does is run his mouth. Davis ain't shit without his boys.* He begins to pat Diego on the back, which startles the champ for a brief moment. Drew was witness to the very end of the drama and approaches the boys with a smile on his face.

Drew-*I heard his boys had hockey practice and he wasn't gonna show up alone.* What a relief it is to hear all that, thinks Diego. *Maybe he went to the dentist to get that dangling tooth out!* The gang laughs it up.

Gabe-*I woulda knocked that joint out for him for a real cheap price.* Gabe looks Drew up and down with a sinister grin on his face. *Drew, where you been anyway, with Alicia?* He shakes his head up and down. He was in the stairwell with his girlfriend making out. The guys always mess with him because his girlfriend is about five inches taller than him and when they kiss, she insists he stand on one stair higher than the one she stands on so they can be the same size. Drew is a bit embarrassed by this, but he'll do whatever it takes to make out with Alicia, so he gladly takes the ridicule. Drew, whose real name is Andrew, lives with his family; it consists of two brothers, one sister, and both of his biological parents. His parents work hard and are trying desperately to get the family out of the projects. Drew's oldest brother is a member of a gang and they don't want the others to fall victim as well. Drew is very skinny and he has yet to grow into his size 10 feet. His shaved head gleams in the sunlight, so he covers it with both a bandana and baseball hat. He secretly wants to be an insurance agent when he gets older, however, when he learns exactly what an insurance agent does, he will quickly change his mind. He is scared of people with gaps in their teeth and British accents. He has grayish/blue eyes and a nervous habit of blinking a lot. Sometimes he blinks over and over again so rapidly that he consciously closes his eyes tenaciously and rubs them in an attempt to control it. He also has some facial ticks that usually get worse when he gets anxious or nervous. All this makes Drew quite self-conscious. Another source of embarrassment for him is that his clothes are hand-me-downs from all his siblings, not just his brothers. At the moment, his pants are way too big and he cinches it all together with a belt. But luckily, at the moment that is the style. Oversized shoes, however, is not the style, so he walks carefully and meticulously as not to trip over his own feet.

As Diego wipes his forehead with his sleeve for the last time, they walk together towards the busy street. They hear someone yell from behind them and Diego whirls around in an instant of terror; he is relieved to see his friend Allan and not his opponent on this afternoon. Allan runs up to the other guys with his scarf flapping in the wind behind him. He slips in some snow and falls while the others laugh at him. Allan is 13 years old and lives across the hall from Drew. His mother would tell you that he came out of the womb saying, *I didn't do it!* He is an albino and is on the receiving end of many jokes at school. The other kids can be cruel and they call him *Al Bino, Al B. Sure, and Alby.* Recently the one that has been getting the most laughs is *Alby needing some sunscreen.* That, however, is about to change because he is about to empower himself and remove the ammunition from the rest of the school. He lives with his mother, step-father, and younger brother, Shelly, who is mildly mentally retarded; his biological father is in jail and has been for six years. He was charged with attempted murder. Jealousy was his downfall, and he let it take over. He thought his wife was cheating and would not stand for it. She was always faithful and was working overtime at a 24 hour diner to help with bills. A confrontation ensued at her place of former employment, and things escalated to the point where he simply just lost it. After three years, their mother finally allowed herself the opportunity to meet someone. When she did, he was the nicest man she could ever meet; he loved her and the boys as well. Shelly requires some extra patience and attention and this man is so patient and tolerant; he loves the boys like they were his own.

For some reason, Shelly is always sweating. He has a slight stutter and walks visibly different than the other boys. Allan is the smart-alecky one in the group, always joking and being sarcastic. He likes to say long words while burping and dislikes people whose breath smell like guacamole.

Drew-*Where were you? Didn't you hear bout the fight?* He bends over to make a snowball, and then wings it directly into a street sign. Cruz marvels at his accuracy.

Allan-*Yea, but I was in the principal's office. Bruce called me Al Bino in front of Mary Pierce again and I said his mother was a crack whore.* The others begin to laugh. *What happened anyway?* They explain all the details that there was no fight; now they are about to take a short walk to Allan's little brother's school since Allan is responsible for making sure his brother arrives home safe and sound. *Yo, let's skitch!*

Skitching is the city version of skiing and hitching all in one. If there was an urban Olympics, it would definitely be an Olympic sport, and the guys would be competing for the gold. As a car passes by, you grab onto the bumper and ski down the street with just your sneakers or boots, unbeknownst to the driver. Some more experienced skitchers may grab the door handle on the driver or passenger side and glide. This usually makes the driver aware of your presence however. They all agree it's a good day to skitch and make their way to the street. They glide across the frozen street and wait for their moment and meticulously choose their target.

Allan-*Yo, Drew, your shoes are so big, you could ski down the Swiss Alps without any skis.* As the other boys laugh, he grows more serious and has a request from his friends. *I want you guys to call me Alby from now on.* The others look on confused. *Well, I've been thinking…Like Fat Joe, he calls himself fat so nobody really makes fun of him for that, so if I call myself Alby then I'm already saying that I'm an albino and so what.* In essence, he explains that he is going to embrace the name and empower himself; within no time whatsoever, everyone will get used to the idea and then won't be able to pick on him for being an albino. The others think it is a good idea and agree to the nickname with very little convincing. Sirens suddenly blast into the guys' eardrums as two police cruisers go screaming by at full speed. All the guys give it is a brief moment of their time before they are brought back to the moment at hand.

<u>Diego</u>-*I heard you guys made some pizza in teen living today, how'd that turn out?* He asks Cruz with a deviant smile on his face. Now that his trauma seems over, at least for the moment, he can enjoy his friends' company.

<u>Cruz</u>-*Shit, that pizza came out pretty good, I had three slices.* He seems proud of his efforts, unaware that he ate some Ivory soap. Gabe and Diego look at each other and bust out laughing. He looks at Drew and sees a big stain on his jeans. *What happened to you?* Drew has a huge stain on his pants, which by the way are two sizes too big. He always gets his siblings' pants, shirts, and sneakers. He has never had anything new, and has also never complained about it.

<u>Drew</u>-*Someone threw chocolate milk from the third floor, when I was walking to homeroom this morning.* They all begin to laugh, Alby especially. Alby and another friend named Lexx were playing milk tag in the halls this morning. If you throw a carton of milk and it explodes on a wall or floor and gets some milk on the other's clothes, then they are it; for some bizarre reason, the game is more fun with chocolate milk. If you use skim or 2% milk, you could be considered a sissy. Alby was thinking he was hitting Lexx, when actually he hit his boy with some chocolate milk. He just found this out for the first time and is having such difficulty keeping the truth hidden.

<u>Alby</u>-*Looks like you're it then, son.* They all laugh some more.

<u>Drew</u>-*Ha, ha, muthafuckas... I think I know who did it anyway. I got him back. I think it was Lexx, so you know what I did. You know how they're fixing the road in the back of the school?* They all listen as Alby can barely keep his laughter hidden. *Well, I found this dead rat, and it was fuckin huge, so I threw it in the road and the steamroller flattened the shit out of it, then I took it and put it in his locker, sliding it through the cracks. He's gonna have a nice stinky surprise waiting for him tomorrow.* He smiles from ear to ear, his teeth showing proudly. His blinking increases and he closes his eyes and squeezes them together tightly. Once again, they are hysterical laughing, especially Alby.

Snowgoons- "Get Down"

Before they begin skitching, they walk four blocks to the public school to pick up Alby's little brother. Shelly has some peculiarities: he likes to watch telethons in Spanish and used to like to chase strings just like a house cat; his brother found that out quickly and whenever bored, would pull out some string to watch his brother chase it and laugh out loud. He doesn't trust people who look like the singer, John Legend. Drew looks at Shelly and notices he is sweating under all of his winter gear.

<u>Drew</u>-*Man, it's cold as hell out here, why are you sweatin?* Alby sees an opportunity to get some laughs.

<u>Alby</u>-*Yo, he's always sweatin, he even sweats in the shower!* Alby explains to Shelly that they are going to skitch, so he wants him to be very careful. Shelly nods in agreement and firmly walks behind his older brother. He tries to grab his hand, but Alby quickly slaps it away making Shelly become visibly despondent. Traffic is backed up on the avenue, as they all get behind an SUV and grab hold. When the light turns green, the driver gives it some gas and has to wonder where the get up and go is. He has no idea that a group of teenagers are getting a free ride. The SUV takes them a good three miles before they let go and walk the other two miles home. Shelly continuously deviates between a walk and a skip as he stays directly behind his big brother. On their walk home, they discuss things they learned in school today. Among them, is the country of Korea. They learned about where it is located in the world, the demographics, imports, exports, and history. It is astonishing how much they remember about the subject as they discuss Korea.

As one gets older, one looks back and reminisces over many things. Soon, however, one notices that some things have changed while others have simply ended. Can you remember the last time you just joked around with your childhood friends? Can you remember the last time you told your father that you loved him? Can you remember the last time you laughed uncontrollably over something so trivial or silly that it was painful to stop? Can you remember the last time you felt extreme anxiety over wondering if that someone special you could not stop thinking about, liked you back? Can you? If you knew at that precise moment that it would be the last time you would do any of those things, feel those feelings, think those thoughts, would it change the way you approached it? Would you relish the situation, savor the

9

moment, make that here and now last forever? For the guys, a lot of what they are about to experience is going to be for the last time, the very last time. Of course, they do not realize it; how could they? Some of those things will be forgotten and never missed, even for a second. Others, however, will be looked back upon with such nostalgia and fondness, that it will be emotional and touching, even to an outsider.

"Marvin Gaye- Inner City Blues"

The boys live in a housing project in the Bronx, New York. Although to some, it may look pretty intimidating from the outside, to them it is all they know; it represents home. It is where they procure love, attention, and are given the basic necessities of life. At the moment, three police cars are outside and someone is in handcuffs. Last night there were shots fired and today an arrest has been made. An alleged drug deal gone sour left one man dead and two others wounded. One of the alleged shooters is being arrested and the police are interviewing the neighbors to identify the other guilty parties. In this neighborhood, unfortunately, cooperation with the police is frowned upon. Not only do people fear retaliation from hoodlums, they simply do not trust the police. It is something that has been inborn in the people around here and many other places all over the country.

Cruz-*Ain't that Tuggle up against the car? They got him apprehended.*

Gabe-He looks at Cruz like he's weird, but knows he likes to practice vocabulary words whenever he can. *Yup. You won't see him again till he's 21 at least. And would you stop using white people talk you fool, you sound like a cop.* He is just joking with Cruz and they all know it. Without too much remorse, they all look on with a hint of sadness on their face. However, this kind of scene is all too familiar in this kind of neighborhood. The boys have gotten hardened over time like calloused hands working construction over an extended period of time. Even though they are all under 15 years old, they have seen this type of drama all too often. Tuggle used to be one of the group, they were six tight, until he got caught up trying to make that quick money and started selling dope. There is never a shortage of the demand for drugs, so more and more young people fill the need to supply it; normally, with horrible consequences in one way or another.

Tuggle's downhill slide began shortly after his father was sent to Afghanistan. Actually, he had been a very good student and somewhat of a homebody. He and his father were very close. Gradually, without his father's guidance, he fell into a pit that he never was able to climb out of. Gabe remembers that Tuggle always carried a sharpened fork in his pocket. The reason was twofold: One reason being so he would always have a fork whenever the occasion arose to have a hot meal since his family always had plastic ware. The other reason being he could use it as a weapon. Once his father was killed in action, his will to get out of that trench was gone forever. The guys remember the day his family received notice of his death. They were playing stickball on the side of one of the buildings and everyone saw two army officers dressed up in pressed uniforms approaching. Moments later, a bone-piercing shrill was heard and the boys ran towards the commotion and put two and two together. From that moment on, Tuggle was never the same, and no matter what the guys did or said to him, it made no difference. It was like he was stuck in quicksand and he was struggling in it as he sank faster and deeper. Gabe was closest to Tuggle, whose father dispensed many kind words of advice to Gabe when he truly needed it and was at a crossroad himself.

Some even concluded Tuggle had the stuff to be an elite baseball player. Gabe remembers Tuggle at his door early Saturday mornings with a mop handle ready to play stickball. They would go to the back of one of the buildings and with a rock, draw a square representing the strike zone. They would use an old tennis ball and within an hour, there would be another six or eight kids ready to participate. Tuggle had a wicked curve ball and Gabe always struggled to hit it. The day they told Tuggle about his father's death, Gabe internally sensed a decline was inevitable; he has an uncanny gift of knowing when somebody is headed for a downfall.

Coincidentally, across the courtyard and in the distance, two neatly dressed military personnel step out of a white Jeep Cherokee, fixing their hats. Around this area, they are known as the *Grim Reaper*, since all they bring is bad news and heartache. When Tuggle gets a glimpse of them, he loses it and begins to resist the police officers. The guys see it coming and can't bear to watch. Gabe turns his face and looks to the sky as Tuggle kicks one officer and spits on another. Quickly, they put an end to his struggle; they overpower him easily as two more officers rush over. One pulls out pepper spray from his side as the other puts his night stick against the boy's skinny neck. They do not see the Grim Reaper across the courtyard and have no idea why he suddenly lost control and became resistant, nor do they care. One officer sprays pepper spray in his eyes and he goes down like a prizefighter who has been taking a pounding. Tuggle continues to scream and shout but his struggle is soon over as they hogtie him with handcuffs and toss him not very gently in the backseat of the squad car. Tuggle thinks of his family and is mad at everyone who he feels has robbed him of his father. At the moment it is the police and they continue to hear his rants. Nobody bothers to ask him why he is so angry, however, the boys know full well.

Curtis Mayfield- "Little Child Running Wild"

The guys continue talking about Tuggle and what happened to him. They are all bummed out about it and wish they could help.

Diego-*You guys remember the poem Tuggle wrote in English? That shit was dope!* Cruz and Drew shake their heads and agree.

Gabe-*Yea, I remember it, I was there when he wrote it.* Gabe reflects back to when Tuggle was struggling with his emotions and their English teacher encouraged him to write it down. He did and read it for class the following day. It was entitled, *What am I supposed to do?* They all remember the poem because it truly hit home for them. They tried to talk sense in to him at the time. Each and every one of them told him hanging with those knuckleheads was going to be his downfall. Now as they walk down the slippery street, they discuss the pitfalls that lay out in the real world for them.

Slaine- "Night after Night"

No doubt
Dealt a bad hand
A whole lot of nothing
I could play it or fold
Folding means losing
Incarceration, addiction, six feet under
To play it would mean fighting
Actually working

Never gonna see my father again
He must hate me
My mother beat me
I must be bad
Somebody touched me
It's my fault
Brother is locked up
Three hots and a cot
Friends are drug fiends
Criminal minded
Isn't everybody?
Neighborhood is a war zone
I gotta survive
What am I supposed to do?

Keep it real?
Get a job?
Be responsible?

But I'm mad!
I'm hurt!
I'm cold!
I'm alone!
I'm afraid!

I wouldn't admit it though
It's survival of the fittest
I gotta keep it real
That means keeping my emotions hidden
Like a shoebox of old baseball cards
I don't wanna be soft
I ain't no punk
What am I supposed to do?

Nobody cares
Nobody will help me
Nobody believes in me
What am I supposed to do?

I have continuous nightmares
About my life
The things I've done
The people I've wronged
It haunts me
Keeps me up at night
Scared to close my eyes
I fight the need for rest
Often, only my tears force me to sleep
I always wake in a cold sweat
Disoriented and confused
Wishing I was somewhere else
Wishing I was someone else
Wishing I was normal
Just for once

Alone with my thoughts
Too much time to think
A true punishment
My own private hell
What am I supposed to do?

What ifs race through my mind
What if I stayed in school?
What if I listened to my grandmother?
What if I hung around better people?
What if I allowed somebody to help me?
What if I believed in myself?
What if I wasn't so insecure?

I don't want to be an old man
With a bunch of what ifs
Dreams unfulfilled
Never even attempted
I can't afford any more regrets
I have too many already
They stab me in the heart
Open my eyes
Make me older than I care to be
I've missed out on so much
I've robbed myself
I've stolen something that can never be returned
What am I supposed to do?

I'd rather have memories
Good ones
I'd like to be able to sleep at night
In peace
Feeling good about myself
Finally
And dream of a future
At least a tomorrow
What am I supposed to do?

The Roots- "I Remember"

At precisely the same time, on the other side of the courtyard unseen by most residents, are two army recruiters talking to some high school seniors. As they talk out in the open, an older woman perhaps in her late 50's confronts the recruiters.

<u>Woman</u>-*You have got to be kidding me! Don't you have enough of our young men over there?* The men are well trained officers who have seen combat themselves. In spite of this, they are unsuspecting and surely unprepared for such an attack like this; they search for words that their training has not yet provided. *I just saw your counterparts on the other side of the projects coming to tell yet another poor family that their father and husband were killed in the war! Isn't it funny that as soon as we lose one, you boys are up here trying to replace him with another? Can't you even give us a minute? How dam insensitive are you?* By this time, a small crowd has gathered and the recruiters have stunned looks on their faces and are dumbstruck; they have no answers. The woman, however, will not be denied her say today and continues. *Why don't you go over to the suburbs and recruit some of them rich folks to go over and fight? Go over to Wall Street and get some of them brokers to enlist their sons and daughters. Why do you think us poor people are so desperate to get out of the ghetto that were willing to give you our lives?* The people watching are in agreement and begin shouting support for the woman. The recruiters attempt to explain their position, but nobody is willing to listen. They stumble over their words and all they do is make things worse. *Nobody is buying what you're selling. Peddle that bullshit somewhere else! You've got enough of our young people, enough of our black people, enough of our poor! Don't come around here anymore! Just because we're poor doesn't mean we have to take the crumbs! We're sick and tired of getting the crumbs!* The crowd shouts and cheers and is in full support. The recruiters retreat, knowing they have no chance today, and quickly walk back in the direction of their car. They simply look at each other and realize today is not their day. They pick up the pace wondering where in the training manual was this subject.

Kool G. Rap, Cypress Hill, Fat Joe, and Big Pun- "Wishful Thinking"

As the boys begin joking around, they hear someone shouting for them from quite a distance away. It is Brianna; she is both one of their classmates and neighbors. She used to live in Queens, and since she has lived here in the Bronx, she has been trying to infiltrate this group of boys for some time now. However, they have been rather resistant to letting a girl in. They could possibly remind one of the *He-Man Woman Haters Club* from the *Little Rascals*. Lately, however, they have been warmer to her. Probably because she takes no junk from anybody and stands up for herself and other people; the boys can relate to that. People call her Bree for short, but the boys have nicknamed her Brixx. They say she is Bree X, like Malcolm X. When she gets angry, she gets very militant and spews violent rhetoric and becomes aggressive and intimidating, even for boys. So, they shortened Bree X to Brixx. Actually, she likes the ring of that and admits it is rather catchy. She is a tomboy and even likes to be referred to as a boy. However, her body is not agreeing with her wishes, and it is now becoming obvious that she is a girl. At over 5 feet now, she has long auburn hair, grey eyes and her curves are beginning to extend from her thin frame. At night, before she goes to sleep, she likes to have her ears covered by her hair to protect her from bugs or mutants crawling in. She knows this sounds crazy but it makes her feel better. She also secretly likes to read other people's greeting cards, especially birthday cards. When she eats a sandwich, it must be cut diagonally or else she will not eat it.

<u>Brixx</u>-*Hey guys, wait up!* She tries to catch her breath while running full speed. Her long hair is tucked under a grey winter hat. She says she runs faster with her hair up; it is squished under the hat like a hoarder hiding newspapers under the bed. Alby looks around and sighs; he is the last one of the guys to warm to her. Yet and still, she has a lot more in common with the boys than they are aware of. Even though all the kids are from New York City, Brixx is originally from Queens while the others have never ventured out of the Bronx, ever. People talk about culture shock, but what is unknown is that people get culture shock in the city, from the different boroughs and parts of the state. Staten Island has a bit of a different accent and slang than say Brooklyn. Manhattan has different lingo and ways of expressing themselves from say Long Island. It may not be as contradistinctive as say London to Texas, or Rio de Janeiro to Atlanta; however, there are still subtle and

obvious differences. The guys give Brixx grief whenever they get a chance. Alby, in particular, is good at sticking it to her.

<u>Alby</u>-*Hurry up, man you people from queens walk so dam slow!* He smiles at her discomfort. Yet she gives it back with the quickness.

<u>Brixx</u>-*Well, when you are from Queens, you **are** a Queen and should be treated as such.* She walks closer and right in Alby's face. Looking down, she gestures for him to bow. *So why don't you bow for me you little man!* She swivels her lips and waits for a response however, there is none. The others just shout *Oh!* As a result, they pretty much make it impossible for Alby to respond. His face says it all as he knows she won this round, but the battle is far from over.

Madeleine Peyroux- 'Weary Blues"

Brianna just turned 13 and is the youngest of five children; she is biracial. Her mother is from the island of Jamaica and is slowly going blind; her father is Russian and remarried, now residing in Staten Island; he rarely visits her. Two of her older siblings are much older and have moved out a while back. Her other two older siblings recently moved out to live with their boyfriends. As a result, she is alone with her mother. Not that she minds this; on the contrary, she loves it. Now she gets her mother all to herself; she gets all the attention, something she only got scraps of over the years. She used to feel like that little neglected piglet that watched and waited while all the other piglets fed voraciously on the mother pig. Even though she is resentful of this, she does not and has never taken it out on her cherished mother. The guys call her a momma's boy and she relishes it; she loves her mother dearly. She always has a scowl of resentment whenever anyone attempts to usurp her time with her mother.

Each and every night, she reads to her mother no matter what. Not a day goes by where she doesn't read at least a few chapters of a book to her dear mother. There are however, moments where she misses her father; nevertheless, she is determined to get past him. When she was seven years old, there was some alleged domestic violence in the home in front of the children, and she was removed and put into foster care by the Department of Social Services. She was in foster care for almost a year, until she was returned to her mother. Although the foster family was kind, it was not the family environment she had become accustomed to; it was new and not normal as she would define it. As a result, she rebelled, ran away and became quite defiant. This is when she began to have anxiety; she dealt with it by having some bizarre mannerisms and thoughts as were mentioned earlier. It worked for her, though, and her anxiety level is now rather low. Her parents could not come to an agreement and her father finally left and eventually started another family; to her, he just washed his hands of the family that he had and was responsible for, and just started over without any repercussions, without any second thoughts.

If he would rather start a new family and be with them, than be with the family he already had in place, to hell with him. That is the source of her anger and she has a lot of it. Even though she channels it in the right direction, she has her weak moments. She is fully aware of this anger, but has no interest in curbing it. She went to counseling for a short while, but exhausted every psychotherapist in the Kings and Queens county area; she was resistant, distrustful, and thrived on confrontation. Often, she would turn the tables on the therapists and question them, making them feel awkward and introspective. She even had one therapist contemplate and then put in for early retirement.

Her motto is it's a tough world and you have got to be tough to make it through. Her anger is strictly directed at her father, never her mother. She doesn't understand why he would want another family because her mother is the best person in the whole wide world.

Susie Hanson- "Blues con Fuego"

The neighborhood is full of characters that everybody recognizes; some are good people and others stick out like a sore thumb. They pass a man simply known as Flip-Flop. He always wears flip flops, no matter the weather. Today, not unlike any other, he is wearing a pair of flip flops. Yes, he is wearing socks, but sure enough, the blue plastic flip flops stand out as usual. It is so common; nobody really remarks about it much, they just say, *What's up flip flop?*

There is a guy in his mid-20s named Eddie who repeats everything someone says in a conversation. He is Eddie Echo. For instance, Brixx was telling him she was going to get the newspaper to read to her mother one day and he responded, *Oh, you gonna get the paper to read to your mother that's good.* She looked at him and stated her mother likes the NY Post, rather than the Daily News and he responded, *Yea, she likes the Daily News over the Post, yea.* Brixx just looked at him and shrugged her shoulders. There is a woman who is called Slurpy, because every time she talks, she makes a sluping sound after she finishes and often has to wipe her mouth. It is a bit bizarre, and always makes the kids giggle. Watching this woman and Eddie Echo have a conversation is hilarious. With him repeating everything she says and then her slurping at the end; they both think the other is the weirdo.

Diego says hello to one of his neighbors, Larry. He is known as *Lawsuit Larry*, because he is always suing someone and has a lawsuit pending. Once, Larry walked directly in front of a bus pretending to wave to somebody across the street. He was hit by the bus, broke his leg, and won $47,000 against the city. Another time, he waited outside of a supermarket in the winter. He deposited money in a water machine where you fill up your own gallon jugs of water; he had no bottle to fill. Rather, he let the water spill out and waited until it froze over. When it was nice and icy, and there were witnesses, he walked and slipped on the ice, claiming his back was hurt. Because he had witnesses, he won $24,700. The boys spot the neighborhood prostitute, who always has a bad cough, always; she is nicknamed coffee. As they walk closer to her, they all cover their mouths and begin to cough in unison, laughing behind their covered mouths.

<u>Cruz</u>-*That's one dumb ho, matter of fact, that's gonna be my Korean name for her, wun dum ho!* The boys laugh more and Alby falls on the floor in laughter.

Always hovering around the lobby is Big Sal. Whatever the conversation may be, Big Sal did it, saw it, or invented it. According to him, he played football at West Virginia, opened up in concert for the hugely popular Earth Wind and Fire in a group where he played trumpet, and he invented the term, "Boo-Ya!". He is still waiting for his residual checks from ESPN and its Sportscenter anchors, which he claims stole his catch phrase. He is kind of like the ghetto Forrest Gump; you name it, he did it. He played squash with Nelson Mandela, checkers with Denzel Washington, and once loaned a pair of trousers to Donald Trump. Don't ask him to elaborate; that is a day long story.

There is Semmie. He is from Cape Verde, Africa. He always talks about what he had in Africa: a huge home, new car, beautiful women, state of the art electronics, etc. However, now he lives in the projects like everyone else. How is that? Someone stated he thinks he is Prince Akeem, from the Eddie Murphy movie, *Coming to America*. But in actuality, he is his faithful servant, Semmie, who pretended like he was the prince, but was really not.

Cachao- "Why? Why not!"

Leaning against the building, smoking a home-rolled cigarette is Rusty. His real name is Ted; however, he has been in jail numerous times and has the tattoos to show for it. Apparently, he has his own personal tattoo artist. However, that artist is either not very good or drunk when he does his craft. His tattoos are horribly ugly, crooked, and misspelled; it looks like someone did it with a rusty hanger from behind bars. He wanted a tattoo that said *Never Scared* but it came out *Never Sacred*. Thus the nickname, in full it is Rusty Hanger, Rusty for short.

Bus driver is aptly named because he drives a school bus. Well actually, he only held that job for four days before he was fired for not having a valid New York license. He rides around the neighborhood with a book bag that sometimes weighs as much as eighty pounds. Inside he has about 6 books, a case of soda, and fresh fruit. Then there is Demo. Every movement he makes, no matter how trivial, is done with such precision and care. It is like he is diffusing a bomb on a demolition crew. If he is playing cards, he deals so slowly and meticulously, one would think there was a bomb under the table. That is where the name Demo originated. Julie McCoy is named after the cruise director on The Love Boat television show. She is super organized and likes to organize other people's lives as well. She always tells people the best course of action whether they want those suggestions or not. She always has a sticky pad with her and leaves sticky notes all over the place for people. There is Lobo, who has one big eye and one little eye; Lobo stands for little one big one. When someone talks to her, it is always confusing which eye to look into, the big one or the little one. Then there is EF which stands for eye fucker. This guy looks directly in your eyes and never breaks the gaze. It is like he is fucking you with his eyes. Most people find it creepy to talk to him because he doesn't respect your personal space. He opens his eyes as wide as they can be and seems like he never blinks. The guys are used to it and always get a kick out of EF.

Last but not least there is Isadore Conavallo, known around the neighborhood as Izzy; some refer to him as *Internet Izzy.* He is 92 years young and has a mind as sharp as a scalpel. At age 49, he had a stroke which put him in a wheelchair. On nice days he is outside the front door getting some sun and fresh air; on bad weather days he can be found in the lobby with a book on his lap. He spends his spare time reading and dispensing advice to all the neighborhood residents who seek it out. He knows things like nobody else and is a joy to listen to. Izzy has an uncanny ability to relate to any kind of person whether it is upper class or lower class, black or white, young or old. Someone remarked he is like a human internet with his wealth of knowledge and wisdom. The people who know him treat him like a library and rather than search the internet, they refer to Izzy. Once, Gabe was talking to him and remarked how smart he thought he was. He responded, *I only know about half a percent of what I would like to know.* Izzy loves to listen to Bob Marley songs and baseball games on the radio.

Talib Kweli- "Everything Man"

From somewhere close, a scream is heard and it gets more audible every moment; the Grim Reaper has delivered his message once again. Gabe wonders to himself how anyone could do such a job. He couldn't do it he reassures himself. The owner of the screams is consoled by those around her but there is no consolation in existence that would be of any value at this moment. Once the Reapers finish delivering their rehearsed and standard apology on behalf of the United States Army, they give their condolences and they are totally ghost. They're gone from one family but on their way to the next. The list gets larger and more extensive every day, yet the speech remains the same.

Meanwhile, the army recruiters have been chased back to their car like a cat chasing a squirrel up a tree. The driver fumbles with his keys and they fall on the ground. Nervously, he picks them up while the other waits anxiously for the passenger door to be unlocked. Simultaneously, the woman and her supporters follow the two, step for step. She continues to berate the two for their insensitivity and racism; in actuality, she is not angry at the young men attempting to recruit new cadets, after all, they are just doing their job. She is angry at the system and the government which allows the continued wipeout of the young men and women who are unfortunately without direction, without prospects, and without options who are seen as expendable. The woman shouts until tears roll down from her face. One of the recruiters pauses for a brief moment and considers going over to console her. Immediately, the other steps in and suggests firmly that they leave. The woman follows no further, exhausted and all talked out. One of her neighbors grabs her arm, and with a gentle squeeze lets her know she is by no means alone in her views or feelings; the others support her vocally. She looks around, weak in the knees, and seems completely fed up.

Mos Def- "Lifetime"

From way across the street, Gabe spots an old familiar face about to step foot into the road. Briefly, they make eye contact; Gabe's eyes light up as if something inside of him has been awakened or enlightened. However, the man does not seem to recognize Gabe. Approximately two years ago, Gabe and this man's brother, who is at least a year older than Gabe, were in a fight, and Gabe gave him a good beating. This is the boy's older brother, five years older than Gabe. He jumped Gabe one day when he wasn't looking, removed his Adidas, threw them on the telephone wire, and then held him. After someone brought his little brother to the scene, he let his little brother just whale away until he got what he felt was revenge. After his brother was done, the older boy beat on Gabe until he was badly bruised and battered; Gabe never forgot. Apparently, the boy, now a man, has fallen on hard times because he has lost some weight, a few teeth, and appears down on his luck; that's good news for Gabe!

The boys say goodbye to each other as they all retreat to their respective apartments. Walking up the staircase, Shelly tells his brother about a hearing test they all took in his school today. With his brother directly behind him, Alby lets out a large and thundering wet fart which was sure to have left a stain in his underwear.

Alby-*Did you hear that?* His brother nods his head and waves his hands in front of his face. *Your hearing is fine then.* He begins to laugh out loud as he voraciously jogs up the staircase with his brother following directly behind him.

Walking down the hallway, Alby spots his elderly neighbor, Mr. Rothman. The guys refer to him as Mothman, because he always smells like moth balls. As Alby passes, Mr. Rothman stops him in the tracks and asks him how he is doing in school.

Alby-*I'm doing great, Mr. Mothman!* He cheeses to himself as the man looks obviously annoyed.

Mr. Rothman-*It's Rothman, not Mothman.* He mutters aloud.

Alby-*Ok. Let's go Shelly.* He ushers his brother to the front door.

Shelly-*Hey, Mr. Mothman!* Shelly is unaware of the man's correct name and truly just wants to greet his neighbor. Mr. Rothman removes his glasses and wipes them against his argyle sweater. He continues to squint his eyes as he mutters under his breath in frustration. *It's Rothman, not Mothman…dam kids….*

Alby wipes his feet on the mat outside in the hall before he puts his key in the front door. Shelly runs inside without wiping his feet and Alby quickly has him remove his shoes that are wet and covered with slush. Nobody is home at the moment; his mother does not get home from work until 6:00 pm and his step-father not much later than that. Alby opens the refrigerator and makes two peanut butter and jelly sandwiches for he and his brother, then pours two glasses of blue Kool-Aid. He instructs his brother to get his books out and get ready to do his homework.

Snowgoons- "Who are you"

Gabe walks across the street observing the man talk with a small group of people and the police. Once the crowd disperses, the man departs alone and Gabe is in hot pursuit. Following his prey like a lion after a gazelle, Gabe stays a good distance behind and attempts to be incognito. He spots the man going down an alley and Gabe knows precisely where that labyrinth leads; he knows that alley like the taste in his mouth upon waking. He begins to run around the corner and waits by the exit, looking around to make sure he is completely alone. Calm as can be, his breathing has slowed down enough so he can hear his own heartbeat. He waits patiently focusing more intensely than he has in any of his classes all year long. Gabe listens to the footsteps approaching with keen precision like the Bionic Woman. When he is sure the guy is alone and it is indeed who he thinks he is, Gabe clenches his fists and begins biting his lower lip waiting with anticipation. Time slows down as Gabe's mind wanders to his mother, his past, and now the present. He begins to think about Tuggle and where he is right now, how they used to be one and the same, playful, carefree, and optimistic. Tuggle is alone with nobody on his side, no advocate to lobby for his release, no savior to provide him with guidance or redemption. Gabe shakes the crowded thoughts away like an antique snow globe and quickly regains his focus. As soon as the unsuspecting man steps out of the alley, Gabe hesitates for a hundredth of a second. In that brief time frame, Gabe flashes back to when he took that beating. He was hurt physically and mentally. He was embarrassed publicly and privately. He was bruised internally and externally. Deep down, he just wants to be alone; to be left alone to his own devices and not bother anyone at all. He would love to just be alone on a rooftop, looking at pigeons, staring at the clouds. These are things nobody, only his mother, ever knew about him. His deepest wishes, fears, and desires have been buried deep down along with his mother. The instant that hundredth of a second passes, Gabe makes his presence known and his prey is struck directly in the mouth with what feels like a sledgehammer! **Wham!** Although Gabe is only 14 years old, he has heavy hands and his punches pack a lot of heat. He has huge hands and very large knuckles that look like speed bumps. The guy falls on the ground holding his mouth and grimacing in pain. He looks up to see Gabe who proceeds to kick him in the stomach.

Gabe-*Remember me, bitch!* It is unclear if he is asking or telling him. Somehow, the guy wonders if it is a rhetorical question. Gabe's actions answer his question immediately. Gabe kicks him again and again until he crawls against the wall and then gets up and retreats back into the alley. For a moment, Gabe notices the fear in his eyes which remind him of his own fears. He sees that life has not been kind to this young man and his eyes show the wear and tear of a difficult life and some apparently horrible decisions. This, however, does nothing to dissuade Gabe of his mission. Without any pity, the man gets stomped for what seems like an eternity. Gabe is wearing construction boots with steel toes, not for any construction purposes, just for extra warmth. He debated about it the day he bought them, unsure if that was what he wanted. Today, however, he is glad he purchased them. *I knew there was a reason I wore these today.* He thinks aloud. The young man now seems like just a boy who struggles to get back to his feet. *Wrong play, bitch!* Talking like he is in the middle of a game of chess, a game of wits, he cracks the man in the jaw with an uppercut, launching him back on the floor, this time unable to rise up. Gabe walks towards him, the image now looking like a boy cowering in fear, covering his face, as he makes another fist. *Next time you see me, you betta walk to the other side of the street, no, you betta run across the dam street, sissy, cause if you're ever on my side of the street, you're gonna be taxed…and I'm gonna expect cash, you got me? I'm gonna be like the George Washington Bridge.* The terrified boy wobbles his head up and down about a thousand times, before he looks up. The premature wrinkles around his eyes now multiplied. Before he makes his exit, Gabe snatches the shoes off his feet. *Fuckin' skips… figures you only got some Payless jammies. You owe me a pair of Adidas too, trick!* Gabe stomps on his back one more time. The terrified victim wonders why fate has brought him to this, and looks up to finally ask a question. Three words manage to escape from his lips. However, Gabe is gone and the boy is left all alone. He is too scared to get up; that alley now feels like his mother's womb, and he does not want to leave. He remains in that same spot for about fifteen minutes before he finds enough courage to leave.

Arturo Sandoval- "Guaguanco"

Crossing the busy street, Gabe suddenly stops and reconsiders going back and getting a couple more stomps in. Although he chooses not to, he feels so much better about himself; it has been a long time coming. He does not like to be a victim, and last year he definitely was a casualty. Gabe always preaches it's better to give the pain than to take the pain, that has been his motto in life and he lives by it. That is precisely why when he was convinced to go out for the football team, he chose defense rather than offense; he would much rather dispense pain than receive it. His football career barely lasted one season before his attitude and inability to accept constructive criticism put a succinct end to that.

Feeling taken advantage of is something he will not stand for, and finally the foul taste in his mouth is gone. This will be the last time that Gabe will ever use his fists to settle a dispute, resolve a problem, or get vengeance. When he looks back on this incident many years from today, he will remember it not with any sense of pride or satisfaction, but rather with sympathy and regret. Forgiveness is something he will work on for years. Once he comprehends that forgiveness frees the forgiver, not the perpetrator, he will no longer be a slave to his emotions and impulses; he will remove those shackles and even help others who have suffered similar fates to empower themselves.

However, at this moment he is still feeling energized, and he runs up the stairs, sixteen floors in all, skipping every other step. Huffing and puffing, he opens his front door and his two sisters are already in front of the television doing their homework. He closes the door a bit so it is opened only a few inches and breathes deeply. Consciously changing modes is easy for him; he is accustomed to it and it is effortless. He doesn't want his sisters to fear him or see him as a thug. He realizes, on many levels, he is their big brother and they look to him for many things: tenderness, guidance, support, advice, and honesty. In addition, his father has warned him to leave the street in the street. He understands where Gabe is in life and where they live. But when they are in their home, he wants better for everyone. Gabe fully comprehends that concept and now is in the process of turning theory into practice. One more deep breath and he opens the door and enters the apartment.

Music Soulchild with C-Lo – "Moments in Life"

The streets are now quiet, the neighborhood settling down, and the drama is over for the time being. People are coming home from a hard day's work and are preparing for some peace and quiet, not to mention a home cooked meal. That's not too much to ask for.

Gabe-*Dad said no TV until homework is done.* Suddenly, his metamorphosis from a two dollar thug, into a parental figure and role model begins. Transforming like a football player who spots his children after a championship game, he lets out a big sigh and finally relaxes; he is now in a different environment and can finally let his guard down without any chance of becoming vulnerable and possibly a target. Before he takes his coat off, he walks over and turns the TV off, giving them a glance like they know better. He sees the box of cookies is empty and gets annoyed. *Why you didn't leave me any?* He rolls his eyes and for a moment looks like a small child that has dropped his ice cream in the street. *Man!* He puts his things down on his bed, which just happens to be the couch in the living room. He then goes in the bathroom, the only room in the house where he can get some privacy. He turns on the hot water yet it never gets hot; he washes his face and looks at it in the mirror. He stares at himself for a while and whispers to himself.

Gabe-*He started it, shit! I just had to get some payback!* He continues to stare, all the while having this conversation with his conscience. He struggles to get some of the boy's blood off of his hands as he scrubs and scrubs. Once all the remnants of the blood are gone, Gabe still scrubs his hands attempting to remove something else. He dries his hands and methodically folds the towel putting it back where it belongs. When he walks out of the bathroom, the house cat, Tazzy, begins rubbing up against Gabe's leg. Immediately, Gabe looks down and picks Tazzy up.

Gabe-*Hello kitty, what you doin? Huh?* He strokes the cat and talks to it like a baby. Unbeknownst to many, Gabe has a soft spot for animals and shows a very tender side. Some may find it odd or funny that one minute he can be pummeling a man into a boy in the street and the next minute cuddling a feline so tenderly; however, Gabe has many different levels, all of which are not obvious to all. He sees Tazzy's litter box needs a cleaning and he rolls his eyes. *More shit I gotta clean up... it never ends.*

Tipica '73- 'Baila Que Baila"

Before Drew ever gets close to his front door, he sees both of his brothers smoking a joint in the stairwell. As he walks up to them, they try and hide it from him, but he is not ignorant. He begins shaking his head in disapproval.

Drew-*I know what you're doing…I'm telling mom.* They plead with him not to tell, but he is adamant and runs up the stairwell to his apartment. They chase after in hot pursuit but his speed is no match. Out of breath, he busts in the door and runs to his mother and tells her what is going on two floors below at this very moment. She snatches her belt off like a ninja, and storms out the front door. Drew sits at the kitchen table with a proud grin on his face as he fumbles through his book bag looking for his baseball cards. He loves baseball and has almost all of the current N.Y. Mets players. He started his collection a few years ago and takes pride in maintaining his collection in mint condition. Suddenly his blinking becomes uncontrollable and he begins to rub his eyes. His mother soon returns, enters the room and sees this and tells him to stop rubbing his eyes and focus on controlling his blinking. She is still fumed about his brothers and takes a moment to catch her breath. Drew looks for his sister and remembers she is staying over a friend's house for the next couple of days leading into the weekend. She is an excellent student and has earned the right to stay at her girlfriend's. Drew's parents believe in positive reinforcement. Their manner of punishment is usually taking things away from the children, like electronics and privileges. However, at this moment, Drew's mother is going strictly old school.

Mother-*Sometimes all someone understands is a whooping!* She has restated this more than once, especially when it comes to her two oldest.

When Cruz opens his door, his sister is inside and has just finished cooking dinner, explaining to him that she has to go to work for a double shift soon; she is an LPN and works at the hospital. She likes to rub her fingernails when stressed and gets lost in the smoothness of them. She also studies the cuticle area on the fingernail, and the moon shape above it; some people have ten moons, others none. She doesn't trust anybody who doesn't have at least seven moons on their fingernails. Cruz is used to being alone in the apartment, but his sister always makes sure she cooks him a hot meal before she leaves.

Cruz-*I'm not hungry right now. My appetite has been stifled.* She explains that the food will remain hot for a while but if he doesn't eat it soon, to heat it up in the oven, since they do not own a microwave or any other device to make their lives more convenient. She congratulates him on using his vocabulary appropriately, and then she puts on her winter coat, reminds him to lock the door behind her, and gives him a big hug before she leaves. He reaches in his book bag and pulls out something he made her in art class today. She acts like she was given the Nobel Prize and delicately places it on the refrigerator; it is a boat made out of ice cream sticks which says, *I love you,* in glitter.

Since the elevator is broken, and rarely working, Diego makes his journey up the 16 floors to his apartment. Out of breath, he opens the door and a plate of rice and beans and tostones is already waiting for him (Tostones are fried plantains which taste like crunchy bananas). His grandparents make sure he washes his hands then sits and eats. As he does, they ask him about his day and he tells them, leaving out the details about the fight of course. They always inquire about his day and encourage him to express his feelings to them. They want him to feel loved and like a priority, especially with both of his parents deceased. His grandfather has a weakness for popsicles, and usually eats an entire box at a time, inviting the indignation of his wife. His grandmother plays cards with her friends every Thursday night. Well, in actuality, the game gets cancelled from time to time, and rather than stay home, she goes to the movies by herself those nights. She loves watching a movie alone without having to explain what is going on to her husband. Be that as it may, she still tells her husband that she is going out to the card game.

In the living room of the two-bedroom apartment is a huge floor model television set that has malfunctioned. Directly on top of it, is a much smaller television that actually works. The floor model has not worked in many years and now just serves as a TV stand and end table for pictures, knick knacks and a dusty plant. The couch is over 10 years old; however, there is not a spot on it. That is because it is covered with plastic which protects it. The couch is very uncomfortable to sit on and always makes a racket when Diego fidgets around. It sounds like someone covered in bubble wrap scraping their nails against a blackboard. In the summer, when he sweats from the scorching heat, it makes the plastic stick to his body. His grandfather, who is always listening to the radio, walks up to his grandson and informs him that a snowstorm is forecast for tonight and the weatherman says there might be well over a foot of snow.

Diego-*I hope so! No school tomorrow!* He cannot contain his smile and begins to hoot and holler loudly as his grandfather covers his ears. Not only would a day off from school be nice, but hopefully the bully and the rest of the school will forget about today and he will be totally off the hook. *Are you sure, abuelo (grandfather)?* He makes sure his grandfather was not teasing him, as he digs into his food. His grandmother is in the kitchen, as she always appears to be, cooking dinner. She is preparing a stew with beef and a wide array of vegetables. Even though they are poor, his grandmother always prepares a hot meal. The meat she uses not be the best cut, but it is meat. She often stews it slow and long so it becomes tender and tasty and falls off the bone.

The phone rings and it is Gabe. Do not think for one moment they have cell phones; they have land lines and Diego still uses a rotary phone with the long telephone wire that stretches all the way from the kitchen to his room. Diego takes a big gulp of water then gets on the phone.

<u>Gabe</u>-*Did you hear? It's gonna snow tonight! School might be cancelled!*

<u>Diego</u>-*Yea, I wish!* By now, everyone has heard in one form another about the possible snowstorm. That does not mean that school will be cancelled necessarily, but the boys sure have their fingers crossed. After a few minutes, Diego gets off the phone full of angst. His grandfather is by the window yawning like it is almost his bedtime.

<u>Diego</u>-*Abuelo, didn't you sleep good last night?* He looks on concerned with his eyes wide open.

<u>Abuelo</u>-*Oh, you know, nieto (grandson), your abuela doesn't let me sleep.* Diego looks confused and asks why that is. *Sleeping with your abuela is like being on the B train.* Diego now is even more confused. *There is a lot of pushing and shoving and someone is always snoring in the corner!!* Diego starts to laugh so loudly his grandmother comes in the room and wants to know what all the excitement is about. Abuelo gives Diego the look and they both button their lip. Abuela stares at the two of them and shoots her husband an order, or threat, depending on how one takes it. Apparently, Grandma heard everything loud and clear, as she always does.

<u>Abuela</u>-*Oh, pues (well), you can sleep on the B train, or you can sleep solito (alone) if you want Viejo (old man)…*

Action Bronson- "Imported Goods"

The sun has already exited and by 4:45 pm it is almost dark. As the last glimpses of light trickle against the housing project, it is like a shift change at a popular restaurant. The students and people working all day return to their respective abodes, while the riff raff and parasites that prey on the weak and helpless make their way outside like a roach that confidently comes from behind the walls after the lights have been extinguished. Inside and out, there is graffiti on the walls; but not like the self-expressions of art that radiate and bring a smile to one's face. It is random, disorganized, gibberish that people refer to as vandalism or tagging. The locks on the front doors of the buildings do not work, the lobbies are often occupied by dregs of humanity, and the 90% or so decent, hard working people that reside there are held captive by their fears for their safety. The hallways and stairwells are not cared for; often the fragrance of urine or some other fowl smelling odor resides way longer than necessary. That is why, even though it is the projects, most people transform the inside of their apartments to their castle, their sanctuary.

As night falls over the city that never sleeps, the rain begins to fall and slowly it turns to sleet which in turn, transforms to snow flurries. There was already a layer of snow on the ground from last week, which is turning into slush. Rapidly, these snow flurries change to a legitimate snowstorm; some call it a whiteout. Briefly, the white blanket covers the muck and grime that stands still, and it looks beautiful and peaceful; that, however, never lasts for long. Although the winter puts a decline to crime and violence, there are always a small minority to which another day is simply that, another day. As most people attempt to wind down after another difficult and demanding day, the sounds of an ambulance screeches past followed by what sounds like either a fire engine or police cruiser. These sounds, unfortunately, are all too commonplace; probably with the elimination of these sounds, the residents would be so unaccustomed to it that they would have a hard time sleeping.

Murs- "Lookin' Fly"

At 6:10 pm, Alby's mother walks in the door carrying a pan of baked ziti with meatballs. She works at a banquet hall and is allowed to take the leftovers home to her boys. Alby and Shelly think this is such a treat as they put the plates on the table, gather some silverware, and give their mother a big hug and a kiss.

Mother-*So, how was school today?* The boys tell her about their day as they prepare to eat a hot dinner. *And guess what, that nice man in 14b gave us some home-made granola that we can have for dessert.* Alby explains there is no way he is eating that home-made granola! *Why not? It's got raisins, you love raisins.* Alby explains the man in 14b is nicknamed 2scoops. You've heard of 2pac, well meet 2scoops. Yes, he makes home-made granola, however, what he failed to mention was that he makes so much of it that it sits for long periods of time and rats get into it. They penetrate the canisters containing the granola and defecate in the trail mix. Alby only knows this because the man gave him some granola about a month ago and he ate some. He later told the man the granola was delicious and loved the chewy raisins mixed in it. Well, the man was stunned and stated he doesn't put raisins in it. Once he investigated, he found out it was rat poop. Rather than throw the entire batch out, he kept it and pretended the rat pellets were raisins. Now his granola is advertised as containing raisins. The look on mom's face says it all as she throws the granola in the trashcan with the quickness. Not ten minutes later, their step-father enters the house, gives his wife a kiss and his step-sons a hand slap, and joins them at the table.

Stepfather-*Can you believe that fool 2scoops tried to give me some of that foul granola.* He laughs as she speaks. *Everyone knows there's rat poop in there.* Mom's eyes get real big as they all share a good laugh. Alby's step-father is a janitor at a local high school. He is a diligent worker and works even harder helping to raise these two boys. His own father was never there for him and he challenges himself each and every week to be a solid father for these boys. If he fails, he figures he would just fold to the ground like an old crumpled newspaper. However, he has come to terms with that possibility and continues undeterred. He is patient and understanding, even though he works twelve hour shifts. Somehow, he has managed to leave the stress from his job at the job, unlike so many envious others. He informs the boys that after dinner he wants to check their homework for any errors. He is obsessed with brushing and flossing his teeth and has passed that tooth obsession on to the boys.

Gabe and his sisters prepare the dinner at his home. Tonight they are having macaroni and cheese, chopped meat, and canned corn all mixed together. It may sound weird, but it is the kid's favorite and it tastes so good. Dad does not like canned corn, only fresh corn, so they put some of the macaroni and meat aside before they mix it all together. He enters the apartment just before 7:00 pm and immediately kisses his girls. Gabe feels he is too old for such displays of affection, so he always gives his father a dap (a fist bump). Gabe's father is somewhat hurt by this gesture, but understands his son better than anyone and wouldn't want to interfere with his maturation process on his terms. Before they eat dinner, they bow their heads and say grace. Not that they are so religious, it is just something their mother used to insist upon and it is their way of honoring her and remembering her the way she used to be, not the way she currently is.

Father-*You have that math test tomorrow, right?* He watches his son nod his head who is always shocked at his father's memory. *Well, before you go to sleep, we're gonna study for an hour or so, I'm going to quiz you.* Gabe doesn't like the idea of doing more schoolwork when he is not in school, but his father is a stickler for studying; he only finished 11th grade in high school and wants his son to at least get a high school diploma. Gabe's father loves reruns of I Dream of Jeannie and dislikes when people offer him solutions when he has the hiccups.

In unison, Gabe's sisters tell their father that Gabe was drinking the soda directly out of the bottle without using a glass. That was something that Gabe's mother always got on him for.

Father-*Gabe, C'mon now, you know better...*Gabe looks to the ground and apologizes aloud before giving his sisters an evil stare.

Gabe-*Snitches.* He whispers under his breath. Gabe is not much for snitching, no matter the crime or the criminal. He follows that code of the streets no matter how outdated it may be. He stares at his sisters and whispers jokingly. *Snitches end up with stitches and wake up in ditches...*He peers at them with a sting like a bumble bee. But all they do is giggle, point and laugh at him. He may be intimidating to others outside the home, but to his sisters he is a big softie; that is precisely his intention.

Drew's mother is busy cooking dinner when her freezing husband walks in the door still shivering. He has on a coat that is not warm enough for the brutal winters in New York. At the moment, he doesn't have enough money for a new one; he took the money that he could have used to buy a proper winter coat on a new baseball mitt for Drew and tickets to the Mets game for opening day in the spring for he and his three sons. His son does not yet know the surprise that awaits him or the sacrifices his father makes for him on a daily basis. Unfortunately, unable to see into the future, Drew's father has no idea that one of his sons will not attend the game in the spring.

The family sits at the dinner table ready to sink their teeth into some baked chicken legs, mashed potatoes, and carrots. Just in the nick of time, Drew's one brother comes in the house, but his other brother is absent.

<u>Dad</u>-*Where's your brother?* He is hoping he hears an answer different than what he is about to hear. Drew's brother explains he is in the street with his friends as Dad puts his coat back on and is about to go retrieve him; Dad believes a family should always eat together, no matter what is going on in their lives.

<u>Mom</u>-*Baby, it's so cold out. Let it be tonight, please.* Grudgingly, he agrees because he knows he is fighting a losing battle. Slowly, he removes his jacket and looks like someone who just lost his best friend. His eyes fall to the ground hard like a brick is attached to each one individually. He puts his hands together and blows on them to warm them up. Methodically, he rubs his hands together. The hardest thing for him to admit is that he has already lost his first born to the streets. He thinks how they used to play catch at the park. When his son was just five years old, he would catch anything his dad threw and hung on to his every word; they were inseparable. He was such a proud father, bringing his son with him everywhere. Holding his hand every time they crossed the street, propping him up on his shoulders whenever he had the opportunity, and giving him an abundance of love and affection which was as natural for him as breathing. Suddenly, his breaths become shallow and he has lost his appetite. He looks down to the floor and wishes he could go back to a time where his son listened to him like a god-like figure. As Dad gently places his coat methodically on a hanger, the look of a beaten man is all too obvious.

Chambao- "Lo Bueno y Lo Malo"

After putting the channel on cartoons, Cruz places his bowl of spaghetti and some slices of white bread on the coffee table and eats his dinner. He ensures a coaster is under his glass. Right on cue, his sister calls to make sure he is home and eating dinner. She asks if he did his homework, if his glass is on a coaster and what he wants for breakfast. They talk for a few moments about her weekend off in two weeks and what he might want to do with her, before she must return to work.

Last night at work, a young, handsome doctor who works with Cruz's sister asked her out on a date. Actually, he has already asked her out four times. Cruz's sister is a very good looking woman, striking some might say. She is a natural beauty but downplays it; she never wears makeup or gets all fixed up. Her number one priority in her life at the moment is her brother. She turned the doctor down and explained her situation; she has very little free time for herself. She has not been on a date for a long time. She does, however, have a lover. They get together about once every couple months or so; that's all she affords herself. She puts her own needs and wants on the back burner. The doctor stated he understood but also that it would not discourage him from asking her out again. Little does he know that she will never say yes. That is mainly because of her responsibility for her brother. In addition, she has studied his fingernails already. He has no moons rising above the cuticle line, so she doesn't trust him and he has no chance whatsoever.

Cruz looks out the window to see the snow falling like mad and just like the others, is excited at the prospect of having school cancelled; he understands fully that to cancel snow in NYC there has to be at least a foot of snow and probably some ice. It is not that they don't like school, but when school is cancelled they have great snowball fights and often get their shovels and go to the wealthier neighborhoods to shovel driveways and sidewalks to earn some money; last winter was quite lucrative for them as they earned quite a bit of money actually. Cruz gets on the phone and calls Diego. He always likes to practice his vocabulary on the phone with Diego's grandparents.

Cruz-*Is Diego occupied?* His grandmother tells him he is eating dinner and will call him back. She remembers when Cruz used to sleepwalk because he did it twice when he slept over their apartment. Her concern comes out by questioning if he still sleepwalks. *No, I haven't in a while. I can tell because I don't have any bruises on my*

40

legs 'cause I would always walk into something when I would…um… somnambulate. He says the word slowly, ensuring he pronounces each syllable perfectly. She is taken aback and immediately comments on his use of vocabulary and commends him for being such a voracious learner. Jubilated, he hangs up the phone and lets out a scream, hoping the forecasts for just snow flurries are being underestimated.

Diego's grandparents are on social security. His grandfather still works under the table at a local bodega, a small grocery store in the neighborhood stocking shelves and helping out. The rules in the home and in the grandparents' relationship are clearly defined, there is no ambiguity of what is allowed and expected. Perhaps that is why their marriage has lasted through all these decades. In their world, it is less complicated and simpler. Grandpa reaches for some chocolate milk in the refrigerator. Noticing there is only a glass left, he puts it back since he knows Diego likes chocolate milk. Just one of many self sacrificing acts in the daily lives in this household. Grandma is in her rocker, sewing up holes in Diego's pants. Diego stares at the pencil markings he has on the wall symbolizing his growth chart and can't wait until he finishes eating to see if he has grown since yesterday. Grandma knows what is on his mind watching him gobble his food.

Grandma-*Slow down and chew your food properly, Dios mio (my god). If you want to grow, you have to comer (eat) your vegetables, that's where all the vitaminas are, nieto.* He looks at her and wipes his mouth with his hand. *And use a napkin, Dios mio.*

Grandpa-*If it snows tomorrow, Mr. Albert says you can come to work with me if you want, make a little plata (money).* He looks on hoping his grandson will take him up on his offer. He truly loves having Diego around.

Diego-*If it snows and there ain't no school we're gonna go shoveling, abuelo.* His grandfather's feelings are not hurt, not in the least. He encourages his grandson's ambition, smiling from his chair. His grandmother looks at him for his improper use of the English language and he corrects himself before she has the chance. *If there isn't school, I mean.* Grandma smiles as she grabs the saltshaker and places it out of reach of her husband who is looking in his plate. *Why do I have to speak proper English when you speak spanglish, abuela?* She tells him it is because he is in school, she is not. Out of habit, her husband reaches for the salt and grabs nothing but air. Without saying a single word, he sees his wife has put her foot down about his high blood pressure once again. He stares up to the ceiling looking like a small child whose new balloon has drifted up to the sky.

As the night continues, so does the snow. Alby and Shelly prepare for bed, as their mother walks in and tucks them both in.

Alby-*Ma, you know I'm too old to be tucked in.* He looks at her with his serious grown man look. He has explained that he now wants to be called, Alby, and hopes his mother and the others will take to it and help him empower himself. He is sick and tired of being bullied, even though he is a bit of a bully himself. His mother places an extra blanket at the foot of his bed. *I'm too old for this.*

Mother-*As long as I am your mother, you'll never be too old.* She smiles and kisses him on the cheek. *Sleep tight and don't let the bedbugs bite.* He rolls his eyes pretending he is tired of such a routine; however he knows deep down that it brings him comfort. She tucks Shelly in and kisses him goodnight; he is talkative and she can see he won't fall asleep for a while. As she walks out of the room, she shuts the light and Alby turns over on his side, blankets bundled on top of him. Subconsciously, he smiles and begins to drift off into the night.

Their mother was the most popular and beautiful girl at her school. She fell in love with the bad boy of the school and became pregnant while still in high school. However, she preaches the importance of inner beauty to her children every single day. She has a secret ambition of making cheese sculptures to supplement her income. Their step-dad is a tireless worker who adores their mother. He treats her and the boys with respect. He raises the boys like they are his own, even though he prepares himself for the day where there might be some conflict and one of them might scream, *You're not my real Dad!* That would crush him, yet not make him love them any less. It is hard to raise children these days, there are so many challenges. In addition, his own mother's mantra rings loudly in his ear like the morning alarm clock; it takes an exceptional kind of man to raise another man's children, and he knows it. When he was a boy, he liked to sing and very badly wanted to be a member of a boy band. Every now and then when he is singing in the shower, he thinks what would have happened if.

Al Jareau- "Morning"

Snoring not so gently, Alby is completely knocked out; he is sound asleep as his brother jumps on his bed shouting.

Shelly-*Alby, Alby, Alby look!* Shelly is excited that the ground is covered with snow and also that he has remembered to call his big brother by his new name. *Alby, Alby, Alby…*He shakes his brother with such force that he awakens with paranoia.

Alby-*What? What the…*He barely opens his eyes. Instinctively, he follows his brother's eyes like a border collie chasing a ball. He looks to the window and peers outside. Apparently the flurries that the weatherman reported were replaced by a serious snowstorm. Snow as far as the eye can see is what he witnesses as he jumps off his bed and onto Shelly's; together they jump up and down like they are preparing for an Olympic dismount. Immediately, he runs into the living room and calls Diego. As he runs he shouts aloud happily. *Flurries my ass, that's a dam blizzard out there!*

Diego's grandmother answers the phone and tells her husband to wake their grandson. Cautiously, he goes into his grandson's room and gently rubs his back trying to wake him.

Grandfather-*Nieto, wake up. School is cancelled today; it's a snow day.* That's all he had to hear and he is up with the quickness. Picking at the corner of his eyes, he jumps on the windowsill and has to see for himself; he does not want to be the butt of any prank today. Sure enough, the snow is falling and there appears to be at least twelve inches on the ground from the way he sees people attempting to make their way through it.

Grandmother-*Diego, it's Allan on the phone.* Barely audible on the other end, Alby is yelling his name the way he wants to be recognized now, Alby. However, Diego's grandmother doesn't hear him and passes the phone to her grandson. Once he puts the receiver to his ear, they can barely contain their excitement. They agree to call the rest of the crew and meet up downstairs in front of Diego's building at 8:00am. *Sit down and eat your breakfast before you go scampering off.* Without a fight, he sits down grinning ear to ear and digs in to his rice and beans, fried eggs, and warm tortillas. Davis and that snaggletooth will not be an issue at all today, that's for sure.

Sleeping soundly on the couch, Gabe is awakened by his two sisters arguing in the living room. When they notice his eyes open, they tell him the news. He jumps up and runs to look outside. The window is so filthy that he can't tell if it has snowed or not, so he opens the window and is immediately slapped in the face by a cold gust of wind. The steam from his breath is apparent. As he peaks his head out, he sees he was indeed not lied to. Expeditiously, he pulls his head back in, closes the window, and runs to the closet looking for his shovel that he bought over the summer because it was on sale. After a few moments, he discovers his treasure and places it gently by the front door like a newborn puppy. The phone rings and it is Diego; the main plan can now be set in motion. He gets on the phone and they agree on a meeting place and time. Meanwhile, his sisters have made some cheese grits made with government cheese. Most people think grits is a southern thing, however, since it is cheep and filling, it makes a decent breakfast and is found in many homes in the north as well. His father gets government assistance and part of that is they receive a block of government cheese and a huge box of powdered milk. The cheese is hard but is good for grilled cheese sandwiches. Gabe passes on the grits and makes himself a double-decker grilled cheese sandwich.

Gabe's father is already at work; he signed up for a double shift today that began at 4:00 a.m. Last night his coworkers asked him to join them for a couple pitchers of beer after work. Instead, Gabe's father chose to get some sleep and come back bright and early to work another shift. He is very involved in his children's schoolwork and checks it daily. As a young man, he was a member of the Black Panther Party in the late 1960's and passed down black pride to his children, as well as self-esteem, and self-acceptance. Just the other day, he helped his daughters on their book report on socialism vs. capitalism. Gabe found it confusing that the United States is a democracy, yet he feels the theories of socialism would be better. Gabe joined in on the discussion as well.

Gabe-*Dad, wouldn't it be better if everybody had a house, a job, and could go to the doctor if they needed too?*

Dad-*Why do you say that?* He challenges his children's brains every day and encourages them to think independently.

Gabe-*Well, if everyone had a home and a job, maybe less people would be criminals… and if everyone could go to the hospital and get medicine when they were sick, they could get back to work sooner to help their business… wouldn't people be happier than they are now?* Gabe is no dummy and these questions prove it to his father.

Dad-*I don't know, son, why don't you bring it up in school to your teachers. See what they say.* He smiled to himself, validating why he works extra shifts.

Eddie Palmieri- "Nica's Dream"

Cruz wakes up to the sounds of his sister in the kitchen. With sleep still in the corner of his eyes, he wobbles into the kitchen to see a big stack of fluffy pancakes, his favorite.

Sister-*Hope you're hungry...and thank you again for the beautiful card.* He walks over and gives her a big hug. Before she asks a question, she already knows the answer. *Are you going shoveling today?* As he shrugs *Yes,* the phone rings and Alby is ready to give him the itinerary. *Well, make sure you put your plates in the sink and be home before it's too late okay?* He answers in the affirmative. *Okay, I'm going to sleep. And make sure to brush your teeth, your breath is disgusting!* She just worked an extra-long shift. However, instead of going straight to bed, she first made her brother breakfast and checked on his well being.

Drew wakes up and looks at the two other beds in his room; one of his brothers did not come home last night. After he uses the bathroom, he walks in the kitchen and hears the good news.

Mom-*Well, there's no school today. What are you going to do?*

Drew-*We're going to make some money, mom!*

Mom-*Dumb question. Well, eat some breakfast first.* He grabs a bowl and a box of corn flakes and plops down in front of the TV. Gabe calls him and tells him to be downstairs in 30 minutes. Precipitously, his missing brother walks through the front door and immediately is bombarded by an interrogation from his parents. Drew is just glad his brother is finally home and not in the streets. *What could he have been doing all night in the snowstorm*? Drew wonders to himself. He also grabs a bowl and sits next to Drew as he passes the box of cereal.

Brother-*You goin to get paid today, little man?* He shakes his head proudly. *Yea, we used to do the same. You know you gotta go to dem rich neighborhoods, don't you. They got plenty of long green to go round!* He looks up to his big brother and would do anything he told him to do, within reason. He pumps him for information on where to go and how to maximize his earning potential today.

Drew's father is an alcoholic, but sober for three years now. He attends meeting regularly. He feels his drinking is the reason his sons are getting out of hand; he holds himself responsible for his children's decline. As a result, he has become very religious and wants the family to go to church every Sunday. Drew's mother teaches them to question everything and not to settle for what others say. Whenever they don't question something, she always says, *I got a bridge to sell you…or I got a guy who can get you anything you need…*Last Sunday, before church, they got into a discussion about church and gangs. Drew wanted to know why people join gangs. After much prodding by Drew, his brother told them that the reason people join gangs is for a sense of belonging, to be with someone who thinks like you, and for a sense of family, since usually they have no family or don't feel connected to their family either by abuse, neglect, or indifference. Drew then asked his father why people join a church; his answer was basically the same. Then he asked how joining a gang and joining a church are different. He paralleled that when people fall on hard times, they reach out. The reason people join gangs and get ultra-religious is because they might have hit rock bottom and need to belong to something where they won't be judged, ridiculed, or looked down upon, and all the while be supported. Drew's mother encouraged the discussion and his thought process as his brother and father couldn't believe the discussion they were having.

Alby is half way out the door before his mother stops him.

<u>Mother</u>-*Uhh, you got to take Shelly with you, Allan.* She has a look on her face of condemnation. Her eyebrows vault skyward and her forehead rolls up causing five dubious lines to suddenly appear. He begins looking irritated and wants his mother to recognize his new self-proclaimed name.

<u>Alby</u>-*Alby!* He says firmly.

<u>Mother</u>-*Alby.* She rolls her eyes.

<u>Alby</u>-*Ahh, c'mon mom…*He looks disappointed that he has to bring his little brother along. He knows the other guys are going to give him a hard time for this.

<u>Mother</u>-*It may be a snow day for you, young man, but your father and I have to go to work. You know Shelly can't stay home alone, so he has to go with you…unless you're going to stay home with him today.* Reluctantly, he agrees and he walks back into the apartment pouting. His mother begins preparing Shelly for the blizzard of 1902, putting layer upon layer on him, a scarf and a hat. Shelly is beaming because he can't wait to play in the snow. In addition, he begins sweating profusely under all those layers of clothing. Alby, on the other hand, explains to his brother that they are not going outside to play, but to work, so he better not be dead weight. Shelly looks out the window at all that snow and keeps yelling that there are flurries outside. His brother has to keep correcting him that it is more than flurries, it is a huge snowfall. Shelly can't seem to grasp that idea and keeps yelling the word, flurries. Finally, Alby gives in, and then agrees just to appease his little brother.

<u>Alby</u>-*Yea, flurries.* Already exhausted, he grabs his shovel and looks for something for his brother to use. The best he can do is use some play shovel that is made of

plastic his little cousin left at their home. It won't be much, but at least he can help somewhat.

<u>Alby</u>-*C'mon Shelly, we gotta go!* Mom gives him a look like, *Where's my kiss first,* so he goes over and kisses her goodbye, sucking his teeth because he knows the guys are now downstairs waiting. He notices that Shelly has some crust in his eye and makes a joke. *Dam, Shelly, you got so much crust in your eye it looks like pizza crust!* He laughs to himself as his mother gives him a look. Then he thinks that was too good a joke to waste on his little brother; he should have saved it for Brixx who he knows comes on strong; incidentally he owes her one.

Before the boys prepare to leave for their journey, Drew spots and approaches Izzy in the lobby of the building and asks if it is going to snow again tonight, hoping school will be cancelled again.

<u>Izzy</u>-*It will snow later but not until after supper. By the way, those shoes you're wearing don't have enough traction if you are going to shovel snow…those dark brown boots you have would be better.* Drew looks down at his feet, tells the guys he'll be right back, then runs back upstairs to change his shoes. His mother suggested the same thing and he paid her no mind. However, Izzy suggests it and he doesn't think twice.

Donnie Hathaway- "The Ghetto"

Drew walks down the stairwell anxiously carrying his snow shovel. His pants begin to sag and he almost trips over them because they are so big. At the moment, hand-me-downs are going to payoff because he is going to be the warmest among the group. Since his brown boots are size 13 and he wears a size 10, he is wearing three pairs of socks. The winter coat is so huge it goes beyond his waist. When he reaches the bottom floor, some boys are smoking cigarettes and they stare him down. One boy takes a step forward, looking at Drew like easy pray, and asks him to empty his pockets. He looks at the boy like he is crazy; he really doesn't need this at this precise moment. Instinctively, he starts swinging his shovel from side to side furiously. One boy tells him if he hits them he is going to pay for it. Therefore, Drew closes his eyes and continues to swing, telling them that he is just swinging and if they get hit it's because they moved into his space. Drew moves the shovel to and fro like a knight of the round table with a cumbersome sword. Squinting his eyes, he sees the boys back up and eventually leave; they begin cursing Drew and shout he is crazy. He readjusts his pants, realizing he narrowly escaped an incident.

The posse is round up and ready to ride out, however, there is a stranger among them.

Gabe-*What's he doing here, Allan…er, I mean Alby?* He has a look of surprise on his face.

Alby-*My moms gotta work so I gotta bring him…*He looks noticeably embarrassed. Gabe is not very happy and expresses his concerns.

Gabe-*C'mon, he's gonna slow us up and keep us from earning more paper!* Alby assures the guys that he won't and reminds Shelly to stay close and not wander off. Shelly stands outside of the circle of boys, sweating like a diabetic in a chocolate factory, unaware that he is seen as a burden to the guys. Looking at Drew, Gabe wonders aloud. *Why you so out of breath?* Drew explains what happened as they walk in the fresh fallen snow. For an instant, Gabe considers going to squash that quandary, but he realizes time is of the essence. The boys discuss their game plan and what neighborhood to hit first. They notice Shelly has a play shovel and that's simply not going to work if he is going to contribute to this firm. Cruz thinks he knows someone who has a shovel and is not going to use it today; he leaves to get it as the others wait outside. In the stairwell, Cruz runs quickly, skipping every other step and thinking of a new vocabulary word. He passes a fire extinguisher and decides *extinguish* is a word and it can be used in a sentence. The boys see the local wino, nicknamed Rain man, and they all say good morning. Often, he gets so inebriated that during more than one rainstorm, he has been seen passed out in the street or on the curb, without getting up. Alby worries that one day he is going to drown in the rain. A while back, he was seen passed out in the street during a heavy downpour. He woke up, attempted to get up but just couldn't manage it. He turned from side to side like a turtle trying to hurl himself over. However, he just couldn't do it and simply gave up and fell back down to sleep it off in the rain.

Cruz knocks on the door of a man they call Vanilla Ice. One day, an icicle fell from a building and landed right in his shoulder; he had to go to the hospital and got 18 stitches. He is very pale and after that day was named Vanilla Ice. Cruz explains the guys' dilemma and he happily loans Cruz the shovel. He tells him it's going to take a couple minutes for him to get it out of the closet because it is way in the back, and there are tons of boxes in front of it. Cruz tells him he will gladly wait and thanks him. Coincidentally, Brixx lives across the hall from Vanilla Ice and is looking out of her peephole eavesdropping. With the quickness, she puts her boots on, says goodbye to her mother and goes in the closet for her own snow shovel. When Vanilla Ice finally retrieves the shovel, he brings it to the front door where his friend is patiently waiting. Cruz grabs the shovel and without thinking sings, *Ice Ice Baby* as he runs back down the staircase. For a moment he thinks he is being followed so he stops and turns around. Feeling sure he is safe for the moment, he continues downstairs. Once he returns with a shovel for Shelly, they are now ready. However, Cruz has not returned alone; Brixx is right behind him. Moans are heard from the other guys as they voice their dissention. Cruz does a double take and wonders where she came from. Brixx is more than ready to give her proposal: she acts as if she was up until almost midnight planning her speech. With conviction and feeling, she explains that she is part of the group and can be helpful in many ways. For instance, if people, especially white people, see this group of boys walking through their neighborhood, not only might they never open their door, they may actually feel threatened and call the police. She goes on to elaborate on a hypothetical situation. In addition, she mentions that she is very cute and that can only help business. Alby is already shaking his head and thinks to himself, *She ain't cute!* The boys look at each other after she has finished and really can't argue too much. Drew stares at her and blinks uncontrollably, trying to focus. Brixx notices his blinking and wonders to herself why he blinks so much, but keeps that to herself. She made a strong point and each one is looking to the other to object.

After a moment or two of silence, Gabe walks over to Brixx and looks her up and down. Brixx stands her ground and is prepared to scrap with Gabe if need be. He scrunches his lips, turns back around and walks away.

Cruz-As *long as she doesn't extinguish our profits, it's cool with me...*The boys are used to Cruz's sudden outbursts of vocabulary, but for Brixx this is all really bizarre. Rather than respond to what Cruz has said, she waits for Gabe and his answer. She looks straight ahead and opens her eyes even wider in anticipation of a disagreement. Gabe turns around and plans out a direct route to the train station.

Gabe-*Alright, let's go already. We wasted enough time.* Without any direct eye contact, he begins walking as the rest follow behind quietly. Brixx thinks to herself, *Wow that was easier than I thought it was going to be*, but makes sure not to look too thrilled in front of the boys.

They walk along like a bunch of cowboys in the old west entering a town where not only is trouble expected, but invited. They discuss the events that may lead to them getting paid well, and all the subtle things that other businessmen might overlook. Moreover, the excitement from the first timers is about to bubble over. Anxiety consumes Brixx; however, she appears as cool as the other side of the pillow during a humid July evening, but refuses to let the fellas know about it. It has been decided that since Gabe is the biggest, and looks the oldest, he should be the spokesman along with Brixx, and try to get the best price. Inwardly, she is smiling brightly; however, outwardly, she shows no sign of emotion; she is as stone-faced as a hardened criminal after years behind bars. They pass Eddie Echo who innocently asks where they are going.

Alby-*We're going to make some money with these shovels, whatdya think?* He smirks at Eddie waiting for a response.

Eddie-*Ah, you're going to make some money with those shovels, huh, good idea, huh, good idea!* He smiles at the group as they walk past him in a hurry. Alby asks him what he is going to do today. *I got school tonight so you guys be good, be good.* Alby looks at his group and cracks a joke knowing it is going to get laughs.

Alby-*Shoot, just cause you get arrested for drinking and driving, and now gotta go to a driving class, I don't think that counts as going to school!* The others laugh aloud and even Brixx finds that humorous.

Mongo Santamaria- "Conga Pa Gozar"

As they leave the projects, the sight of untouched, virgin snow captivates the landscape. At this precise moment, every neighborhood looks the same: clean, pure, and unblemished. Rapidly walking to the subway, they see another group of kids from their school that apparently had the same idea as them; now there is competition. Gabe walks quickly but also carefully as not to fall down. Suddenly, a snowball crashes against the *No Parking* sign above his head. He whirls around and no longer sees the rival group holding shovels. Drew notices Lexx is one of their adversaries and would like to get him badly.

Gabe-*Okay, they wanna battles us? It's on!* As the unequivocal leader, he gives the other guys the cue, and suddenly they are packing snowballs and taking cover behind the armored vehicles. Cruz peaks his head out into a barrage of snowballs, which knocks the hat off of his head. *On three…one, two, three!* Abruptly, they appear from beyond the vehicles like a bunch of newly recruited soldiers straight out of basic training. With great aim and velocity, they pelt their rivals from every angle until they are out of ammunition. Once again taking cover, they reload. Shelly stands up and is hit directly in the mouth with a snowball and proceeds to cry. Immediately, both of his mittens race to his mouth and muffle his cries. His brother notices what has transpired and shakes his head, then gives him direction.

Alby-*Oh boy, come over here quick, and stay low.* He comforts his brother and hands him two snowballs. *Throw 'em like I showed you how, you remember?* Shelly nods his head, and attempts a smile, tears still rolling down his sweaty face. Once again, Gabe leads the charge and they attack. Shelly's snowballs do not make it across the street but the guys congratulate him nonetheless. Brixx makes snowballs so fast, she has made an excess of ammunition the others can use without having to stop and reload. With her help, they attack with machine gun-like velocity and quantity. The snowball fight continues, catching some innocent bystanders by mistake until they run the opposition away. Drew, whose dream it is to pitch for the New York Mets, single handedly forced their retreat with his fastballs. Gabe pats him on the back of his Mets jacket and together they are all victorious.

Diego-*Did you see Drew hit that fool, Lexx, in the face! What a throw!* They all laugh and slap hands before they realize time is being wasted. *Yo, time is money, let's get going!* They all grab their shovels and pick up the pace walking to the subway station. Alby wipes away the almost frozen tears from Shelly's face and notices snot forming in the corner of his nostrils. As Shelly breathes, a bubble comes out of his left nostril. When he inhales, it grows larger. Then as he exhales, it shrinks smaller, like a poison blowfish attempting to scare a potential predator.

They walk single file, still armed with snowballs just in case someone else wants to challenge them. Brixx covers the rear, taking her role very seriously. Shelly is happy and keeps screaming, *flurries.* The group tries to correct him but to no avail. Alby explains he already went through that ordeal and it is fruitless. The group doesn't care that much and ends up agreeing with Shelly just to keep him moving.

Cruz-*How much you think we can make today?* He asks his partners in crime looking like a salivating lion.

Diego-*Well, last year how much did we make on a good day?* He stops in his tracks and scratches his head with his gloves on.

Drew-*Shit, we pulled down a Benjamin ($100) each, two days in a row!* He kicks a pile of slush with his boots.

Diego-*Maybe we should bump up our asking price this year?* He notices his fly is down on his jeans and immediately zips up his fly before anyone notices.

Gabe-*Don't get greedy, bro. If we do a good job then people will remember us and we'll get repeat business, that's where the loot is. If we knock out 20 houses today, and it snows again tonight, we can get at least 10 of those same houses again tomorrow.* He explains his business plan like Donald Trump on *The Apprentice.* The others listen on and agree as a dog runs in front of the group and across the street.

Shelly-*Alby! Alby! Look at the dog!* Gabe looks at Alby, concerned about bringing his little brother. Alby tells his brother to relax and be quiet. *I have my shovel too...* He shows the others. *I wanna make some money, too.* The others hope that he is not going to be dead weight and express that point of view.

Once they get on the subway, they see the masses of people going to work and the bland expressions on their faces. Some of the riders see the boys with their shovels and flash a brief smile, recalling better times in their youth when perhaps they did the same. Some of them wish they could trade places; if only there was a magic genie that could appear out of a puff of smoke and grant such an incredible wish.

As the train gets more and more crowded, each and every one's personal space becomes smaller and invaded, until they are pressed up against one another like a family-size package of chicken legs at the supermarket. Alby has a hold of Shelly's hand; he is sweating from under the bundle of clothing he has on.

Shelly-*Alby! I'm hot!* His brother just ignores him and watches the reflection of the people in his shovel, dreaming of the escapades they are going to have today, and thinking of some good jokes for Brixx. The other guys have on a permanent smile resulting from the fact that school has been cancelled. Today is almost like a vacation and they are looking forward to their retreat. Shelly tells his brother about a boy in his class named Dennis who has a southern accent and asks why he speaks like he does. Alby does his best to try and explain it. Shelly finds the accent unique and thrilling, he always enjoys listening to Dennis speak. Gabe listens on as his reservations about Shelly coming have not disappeared. Diego knows what Gabe is worried about and he elbows Gabe in the stomach.

Anthony Hamilton- "Coming From Where I'm From"

Gabe lets them know that this is their stop as they squeeze past the crowd of disillusioned workers on the way to their nine to fives.

Alby-*See ya later, suckas…*He says it out loud to nobody in particular, but also to everyone on the train collectively. He means no harm at all, he is just glad he doesn't have to go to school while the full train must head to work. A few riders on the subway actually took what he said in and process it. Before Cruz steps on the platform, he makes eye contact with a man in a double-breasted business suit whose phone has just rung. The man gives him a nod to which Cruz seems confused.

Shelly watches a man in a three piece suit pass a homeless man sitting on the ground, resting up against the wall; he has a long beard and holes in his shoes. The homeless man raises his Styrofoam cup for some change but the man snuffs him and proceeds past him in a hurry. Running late, he checks his watch and swiftly runs up the stairs to the street. Shelly stares at them both as the homeless man makes eye contact and innocently smiles at him.

Look at them
Digging through the trash
Lugging bags of cans
Looking disheveled
Wearing three jackets
Smelling like garbage
No direction or meaning
No family or loved ones
No stability
No possessions
No wife
Nothing but the rags on their back
How pitiful
I've got so much
Too much to lose

I could never be like that
I try to ignore them
And pretend not to see them
But I do
I really feel sorry for them

Look at them
Rushing to get everywhere
But not going anywhere
Lugging their briefcases to their nine to fives
Looking like it took them hours to get ready
Wearing their jackets and ties
No direction or meaning
Backstabbing friends and coworkers
Disloyal family
Living with their false sense of security
Living in denial
Because they could easily be in my shoes
With just a simple run of bad luck

Worrying about their cars
Sweating over their mortgages
Stressing over their girlfriends
So many things to worry about
How pitiful
I've got nothing
Nothing to lose
How liberating
Total freedom
Not held down by possessions
Or deadlines of any kind
I could never be like them
I see them trying to ignore me
Pretending I am transparent
But I know they see me
I really feel sorry for them

Candido-"It Don't Mean A Thing
If Ain't Got That Swing"

Once they make their way to street level, they appear lost. Each one looks at the other with a puzzled look.

<u>Diego</u>-*Which way?* They turn to each other and then Gabe points the direction, even though he is unsure himself. After walking four more blocks, it looks like they have reached their starting point. Shelly points to a hill and shouts, *flurries*, and they are all distracted. There is a hill across the street and some kids have sleds and are gliding down the hill and screaming with joy. None of the guys have ever owned a sled, or even have seen one in person for that matter. However, they have sledded before, just not with sleds. They all have the same idea: cross the street, take the garbage can lids off of the cans and make their way to the top of the hill. The other kids look at them strangely not sure what they intend to do with the garbage can lids. One by one, they sit on the lid and slide down the hill. Gabe and Brixx smash into each other on the way down and Gabe flips over and finishes the slide on his back. Brixx points at him and laughs. The kids with the real sleds abandon their prefabrications and get themselves some garbage can lids of their own, mimicking the guys. Together, they all sled down the hill screaming and laughing. Gabe brushes himself off, motions for the guys to come together, and attempts to get everyone organized and ready for work.

<u>Gabe</u>-*Okay, let's get down to bizness now. You guys ready?* They all look at each other and agree that play time is over. *As the spokesperson I think first we gotta split up the responsibilities.* Gabe is a born leader and the others recognize this; that is precisely why they voted him the mouthpiece. With the next words out of his mouth, they each are given a role: Diego and Gabe will work from each side of the sidewalk until they meet in the middle, Cruz and Drew will start at each side of the driveway until they meet, Alby will work from the stoop to the driveway so he can keep an eye on his brother, Brixx will follow up each man's work and tidy it up, making sure it is clean, tight and spick-and-span, and Shelly will shovel the stoop. Everyone agrees it sounds like a good plan as they make their way to the potentially first client. Together, they meander up the elongated stoop as Diego presses the glowing doorbell. Brixx looks at the group and quickly dismisses them

with the back of her hand. Diego gets the hint and interjects while Cruz and Drew are fighting for position.

Diego-*Hey, I don't think we should all be up on the stoop.* He puts his hand up.

Cruz-*Why not?* He has a hurt look on his face.

Brixx-*C'mon stupid, think about it. Like I told you before, you don't wanna scare people. Look at you; you look like a bunch of thugs from New Jack City.* She smiles condescendingly at the boys. *Jeez, you fools need a lady's touch.* She takes her hat off and shakes her head letting her hair fall way below her shoulders. The other guys suddenly look at Brixx differently as she cleans herself up so to speak. She scowls at them when she notices their expressions have changed. Diego quickly shakes it off and agrees with Brixx.

Diego-*Because if they see a bunch of kids on the stoop they might not answer the door.*

Gabe-*Yea, he's right, you don't wanna scare the people, you know how easily white people get scared.* A big smile appears on his face.

Drew-*But we're just tryin to work, we ain't gonna rob nobody.* He takes it personally and looks offended.

Gabe-*Well, we know that but they don't know it, so back off.* He waves the others off the stoop so only he and Brixx are in front of the door. Two people are appropriate, he explains, without making the people feel threatened in any manner. This is probably their best strategy to maximize their earning potential today. After another ring of the doorbell, the door is answered but it is only opened perhaps two inches.

Homeowner-*Yes, can I help you?* Only one eyeball can be seen through the crack of the door. That one eyeball rapidly goes from one teenager to the next like a pinball bouncing off one bumper to the next in a pinball machine.

Gabe-*Morning, mam, would you like your driveway shoveled today?* The grin on his face is so fake and exaggerated that Brixx feels like elbowing him in the ribs.

Homeowner-*No thanks; my son is going to do it.*

Gabe-*Okay.* Gabe and Diego turn and join the others walking away. As they walk up to the next door, they chat about how much they should be charging. Diego tells the others they need his magic touch. He rubs his hands together and blows on them, cracks his neck, and walks to the door. As he rings the bell he steps away from the door looking around. Immediately, a young woman answers the door and opens it wide.

Homeowner-*How much?* She can see that the boys are there proudly holding their shovels.

Gabe-He gives the driveway the once over and looks her directly in the eyes. *Twenty bucks.* Without any hesitation at all, she answers back

Homeowner-*If you guys can knock it out in 15 minutes, I'll give you thirty.*

Gabe-*Bet it up!* He looks at Brixx and she gives the others the nod as they jump right to it and get to work. Like a well oiled machine, the boys and Brixx each take their respective position and begin shoveling. Alby instructs Shelly for the second time what he should be doing and keeps a close eye on him. It becomes apparent, however, that Shelly is already consumed about thoughts of placating his stomach.

Shelly-*Alby, I want pizza for lunch.*

Alby-*Lunch? We just ate breakfast.* Shelly stops working and makes a sad face. *Don't stop working. If you do a good job we'll get pizza for lunch, but not till much later, Okay.* Shelly nods quickly and resumes his job with pride. Precisely eleven minutes later, the boys are done. Diego inspects the driveway, sidewalk, and stoop before he rings the bell.

Homeowner-*Beautiful, boys!* She comes outside, closes the door behind her, hands Gabe three ten dollar bills and opens the garage to get her car.

Cruz-*Dam, that was easy!*

Drew-*Right! How much you think we can make today?* Cruz and Drew stare at each other in amazement. Never have they made any kind of money in that short period of time. Their discussion, however, is cut short. Alby watches the two boys who appear to be catatonic and in a trance. With perfect timing he interrupts the moment.

Alby-*You two gonna kiss or you wanna make some more money?* Gabe and Brixx start laughing as they walk to the next house. Three houses later, they seem to be on a roll.

Sting- "Fragile"

Cruz is still needling Gabe who just promised some old lady that he would shovel her driveway for five dollars before they were done for the day. The lady is on a fixed income and can't afford any more. Gabe promised the boys that they would make as much money as they possibly can during the day, and before they boarded the train to go home, they would shovel her driveway last. He even said that if he had to, he would come by himself to do it if the others changed their minds or were too tired. Alby said there was no way he was going to return for a lousy five bucks split among the whole group.

For some reason unbeknownst to him, that old lady reminded Gabe of his mother before she was hooked on crack. They both had pretty hair with streaks of grey in it. In addition, the way that old lady smiled and laughed was similar to the way his mother would smile and laugh at Gabe and his sisters. She was always in a good mood and optimistic. She was so supportive of her son, and he has no idea how she lost her way. He racks his brain and just can't figure it out; he misses her terribly and intends on keeping his promise to that old lady. Walking down the street, he thinks of his mother. Making sure the others don't see, he wipes away a single tear that escaped his tear duct and barely made it past his nose before it was struck down with homicidal force.

For their first hour, they have shoveled four houses and have been told no, only five times. Drew likes those odds as he spots a house across the street with a circular driveway.

<u>Drew</u>-*Yo, look over there!* He points it out to the others and they make their way single file. The name on the mailbox says Taylor. *How much for this one?* Diego looks at Drew and tells him that he better work extra hard today. Drew looks at Diego curiously until Diego responds.

<u>Diego</u>-*Remember, you gotta get me a new MP3 player...mudbutt.* You might ask yourself MP3 player? Well, these boys have never had an Ipod, and to them an MP3 player is a luxury. About three months ago, Cruz, Diego and Drew were taking the train home from his cousin's birthday party and Drew had borrowed Diego's brand new MP3 player. Drew had to go to the bathroom really bad and could not wait to get home. They ate some tacos at the party and it was not sitting

well in Drew's stomach, especially since he put extra hot sauce on each one. They exited the train before their stop and Drew scurried to find a bathroom like an ant with a magnifying glass aimed at him. All the while Cruz was laughing and yelling *mudbutt* at him. Finally, Drew found a bathroom in the back of an auto body shop, and entered the stall. However, someone had already beaten him to the toilet and left a bomb inside without flushing. Drew bent over to flush the toilet and Diego's MP3 player fell out of his jacket pocket and directly into the toilet; a bit of the dew splashed on his new pants. He was stunned, and then figured he would rather buy Diego a new one than put his hand into the nasty toilet bowl. In addition, when he tried to flush it, there was nothing but silence. He tried again and again, still nothing. The water level was already almost up to the seat and he had little time to make a decision, because his bowels were already in motion, leaving him no time to come up with a backup plan. Closing his eyes and hoping for the best, he decided to bend his knees and squat over the grotesque mess to quickly do his business. With a grimacing look on his face, thunder trumpeted as the falling debris splashed the water and himself thoroughly.

Lauryn Hill and Mary J. Blige-
"I Used To Love Him"

I used to do a lot of things
But life was different back then
I was a different person back then
I used to love myself
I was confident, independent, and pretty
I had a lot of friends and admirers
I had my pick of the litter
And look what I picked
Litter

A lot has happened since I was a naïve girl
Now I am not so sure of myself
Codependent and ugly with very few friends
And even fewer admirers
He has seen to that
My choices have dwindled down to zero
I am stuck
With a man who is everything I told myself I did not want
Ever

I used to love him
I used to worship him
I used to want nothing more than to be beside him
I used to fall to pieces whenever he said my name
Like I said
Used to
Now I despise him
Detest him and loathe him
Now I fear him
Can't stand the sight of him
And I cringe whenever he says my name

I wish I could get the pieces back
I'd glue it back together and make it whole again
And get as far away from him as I could
But now it is too late
For me and my child
I am scared for me
But terrified for my child
He would find us and beat us
Perhaps kill us
I know he would
He told me as much over and over
And I believe him

I hate him
If I had an ounce of courage left
One morsel of self-respect remaining
I would take a knife and slit his throat
While he was sleeping
If only I could be sure he would be dead
I would do it
My fear of him having enough strength
Left to do harm one more time keeps me stagnant
If I had just a gram of discipline left
I would take a knife and slit my own wrists
While I take a warm bath
And gently drift away from this prison
If only I could be sure I would die
I would do it
My fear of waking up in the hospital
With him at my bedside
Knowing I had to return to my nightmare
But this time with even less courage and strength
Keeps me paralyzed

People have no idea what he is really like
He is like Clark Kent
Everyone thinks he is an angel
They don't know how he transforms
Not into Superman
But into an evil entity
Someone I have never known
Only have seen on the Hollywood screen
He covers his tracks like the Vietcong
He is a master at infiltration and torture
Psychologically he is terrifying
Nobody would believe me
Shit, sometimes I don't believe me
That is his gift
He makes me doubt myself
And somehow feel responsible
Imagine that
If you knew me years ago
You would not recognize me either
I was outgoing, strong and vocal
Now, he has beaten me until I am nothing but pulp
Puny, dependent and silent
Even in my solace
My cries are mute

When we have sex
I count the seconds until it is over
Again silent in my horror and rage
He has socialized me into a mute
A blind and deaf being

I hate him
I hate our life together
I hate myself
I hate
I

Keyshia Cole- "You've changed"

After they agree on a fair price to ask, Diego rubs his hands together and rings the bell. A tall man with broad shoulders answers the door before he rings a second time. He looks like someone who played football many years ago and has kept himself in very good shape. The dazzling smile on his face inadvertently makes the group smile themselves. As he steps out of his home, Gabe and Brixx are directly in front of him and the personal space invasion bothers nobody in particular. He stares the group up and down and wipes a piece of a bacon and egg sandwich from the corner of his mouth. Mr. Taylor likes to giggle during horror movies, while brand new movie coming attractions make him anxious.

Mr. Taylor-*Okay, how much are you charging guys?* After a little shrewd negotiating, they agree on a price and immediately begin to work. Included in the price, the guys are going to have to shovel out his car which is parked in the street. When the snowplows passed by earlier in the day, they completely buried his car. Drew and Cruz get started on the car, and within minutes they can identify the make and model. Drew's eyes get big and filled with envy.

Cruz-*Wow, nice fuckin' beamer.* He is pointing to the BMW which is in front of him. He makes sure the car is cleaned off and has plenty of room to get out onto the street. Everyone pauses for a moment to gaze at the car. It is dark blue and although it still has a bit of snow on it, it is sparkling on this cloudy day.

Drew-*I'm gonna get me one of dem one day! Watch!* He declares to his homeboys.

Alby-*Oh yea, you gonna sling rocks like your brother to get that loot?* The moment he says it he regrets it as Drew shoots him a nasty look but says nothing in response. For a moment he thinks about his brother, then puts his anger through his shovel and tosses snow up in the air. It should come as no surprise that Mr. Taylor has a BMW because the house itself is monstrous, which is the perfect word since a monster indeed resides within.

Brixx-*I guess you gotta have a car like that to go with the house.*

Cruz-*I know, you can't have no hooptie (piece of junk car or old car) if you live in a phat house!* They all agree as each one of them secretly starts wishing they lived in this immense house and had an elaborate car like that one. One of the guys wishes aloud that he could trade places and live here. As they discuss the life of luxury that exists from the outside, the residents on the inside might have an entirely different perspective.

Billie Holliday- "No Good Man"

Mr. Taylor and his wife are preparing for work and their eight year old son is preparing to be dropped off at his friend's house. As he peers in his closet, he carefully chooses his power tie for the day and meticulously ties the Windsor knot. The tie looks perfect, but not to him; he spends an additional five minutes making sure it is perfectly synchronized. He peers out the window to see the progress the boys have made and he promptly notices his son's bicycle sticking out from some snow in the driveway. In haste, he walks downstairs and opens the front door asking the group for some assistance.

<u>Mr. Taylor</u>-*Hey guys, could you do me a favor and please put the bicycle there against the wall.* He points with two of his fingers. His smile still remains on his face from earlier. Cruz nods and gets right on it. He notices how large of a man the owner of the house is and wonders aloud to his boys if they think he was a football or hockey player back in his day. They all comment on how nice he seems. Diego thinks if his dad was still around, would he be anything like Mr. Taylor? Since he will never know, secretly he admires and looks up to this stranger. Mr. Taylor walks back inside, shuts the door and storms directly into the kitchen. He stares at his son with his arms folded and waits for him to look up from his bowl of Fruit Loops. *Where did you put your bicycle last night?* His son's answer is that he put it in the garage. He moves closer to his son and hovers over him like a morning biscuit covering a sausage patty. *Then why is it still in the driveway covered with snow?* The look on his son's face shows terror as he tries to backtrack in his mind. He begins apologizing to his irate father who just stands there shaking his head, towering over his son. To an eight year old child, he appears gigantic and very intimidating like the abominable snowman. *Is that why I paid $1,200 for that bicycle? So you could just leave it outside in the snow to rot?* The son is unsure if it is a rhetorical question or not, as he gulps twice, making sure not to make any eye contact. *Why don't I just flush my money down the fucking toilet!* He throws his hands in the air and begins to shout as his petit wife makes her way downstairs towards the commotion. As the son attempts to go outside to retrieve said bicycle, he must first pass his father who is infuriated. Miraculously, he walks past his father relieved he did not receive a beating. However, his relief is premature as he is struck in the back of the head and topples over onto the cold floor; he slides a good three of four feet after he hits the floor. His shirt

crumples upward and his bare skin grinds against the cold linoleum, scraping up his elbow and forearms in the process.

Mrs. Taylor-*Jesus Christ!* She rushes over to her son who is now crying and holding his head. Mr. Taylor is now ranting and raving and walking towards the two in the hallway with a slow, steady gait.

Some history is obvious, just never recorded or discussed. Mr. Taylor was a victim of abuse himself; he and his mother were beaten by his biological father and he was taught that is how a man acts. He has learned to equate love and violence in a very unhealthy atmosphere. Mr. Taylor never learned the correct way to express love; he never was taught how to be a man, a father or a husband. He never learned to express his anger appropriately and gradually became a bully at school. He found any way he could to gain power and control, which even included cruelty to animals. This by no means is an excuse, simply an explanation.

Shelly is on the stoop and hears the arguments inside. He looks around; however, nobody else seems concerned at in the least.

Shelly-*Alby, they're fighting!* He walks over to his brother.

Alby-*So what? Who isn't fighting? Get back to work.* He instructs his little brother, ignoring what he said. All the while, he looks at the others to let them know that he has control of the situation, and that his little brother is not going to be dead weight. Alby motions to his brother with his head and lips that he is dead serious. Drew and Gabe begin talking about the aforementioned bicycle.

Gabe-*How much you think one of those costs?* He looks it up and down in between his shoveling.

Drew-*I dunno, but it's gotta be at least a grip (an abundance of money)...more than a few bills.*

Diego-*Yea, you won't see one of those at Toys R' Us, that's for sure.* They all agree as the snow has seemed to let up for the moment. Inside, however, nothing has let up. On the contrary, Mrs. Taylor gets up and walks over to her husband shouting and cursing. Mr. Taylor tries to explain himself, but he loses control once again and strikes his wife across the face as she joins her son on the floor; together they lay motionless.

Mr. Taylor-*I got enough bullshit to deal with without having more bullshit at home! Do I need this, really?* He asks himself aloud, then walks closer to the two and extends his index finger. *Why do you make me hit you? You just ask for it, don't you?!* His son is rubbing his head, trying to hold back the tears and his wife has her hand on her face, afraid to look her husband in the eyes now. *Nobody listens in this fucking house!* He gestures more with his fists, pounding the air. His son gets up and runs up the staircase, which provokes Mr. Taylor to chase him and strike him once again in the back of the head. This time, his son falls to the ground and slides into the wall, hurting his arm in the process. *If I see that bike in the driveway one more time, I swear… It…It would serve you right if one of them kids outside stole it, that would teach you a lesson! I hope they steal it, shit, maybe I'll just let them have it, I bet they wouldn't leave it outside over night. You think they would, I bet they'd appreciate it and take dam good care of it…*His son just lays in the fetal position on the floor crying. Mrs. Taylor drags herself to a chair, terrified to agitate her husband any more.

Mrs. Taylor-*You said last week that it was going to be the last time…*She is already shaking her head because she knows she spoke too soon and probably just added fuel to the fire. Storming down the staircase, he walks up to her and raises his hand but catches himself and resists the urge to strike.

Mr. Taylor-*Yea and you said you were going to control your dumb ass son! Remember that!* He buttons his shirt sleeves and fixes his tie once again, turning back into the nine to five version of himself. As he takes a paper towel and wipes any perspiration on his face, he realizes this episode has thrown off his schedule and he may be late for work. *If I'm late for my meeting this morning, I'll show you something for the last time, you can bet your sweet ass on that one you…*He begins mumbling under his breath as the rest of the sentence falls to the floor quicker than his son did. His voice becomes almost mute until suddenly he tells his son to come downstairs and finish his breakfast. Mr. Taylor walks past a wall mirror, pauses for a long moment to ensure his tie is more than satisfactory. If he feels his tie is spot on, then on some level he believes everything is just as it should be; somehow, it is all interrelated. Noticing it leaning just a bit to the left, he shakes his head and lets out a sigh, unhappy with his family's behavior and lack of respect. He mumbles under his breath one last time, which just works him up a bit more.

Snowgoons-"The Hatred 2"

Without warning, a cold breeze hits Brixx in the back of the neck as she squints to the sky. She gazes as the breath releases from her mouth like a falcon gliding in the sky. Two more times she blows breath from her mouth, puckering her lips in a circle, watching the steam rise thickly; it slowly dissipates until it is completely gone. Suddenly, she realizes her neck is barren, covers it snugly, and tucks the rest of her hair under her wool knit hat as she thinks about her father for a brief moment. Making real sure her ears are concealed, she wonders what he is doing right now and if he is thinking of her or is he too busy with his new family. She wonders if she lived in a house like this, would her father have remained, would her family still be together, rather than just a fragmented shadow of a thousand piece puzzle. Slowly reaching into her back pocket, she pulls out a drawing she did in science class the other day. It is a picture of herself holding a hand grenade standing next to a desk with a microscope on it. She drew it at a moment when she was angry and then crumpled it up and threw it away. Moments later, she retrieved it from the garbage and folded it up, putting it in her back pocket. Her pants have been washed since them and so has the picture. She studies it for a few seconds before shoving it back in her pants pocket.

Diego takes a break for a second and stares at the huge house. He remembers his grandparents discussing the house they grew up in back in Puerto Rico, and even though he is sure they exaggerated, he would like to think that it was something like this palace before him. Gabe notices him staring in disbelief and smirks from having the same daydream.

<u>Gabe</u>-*Maybe if you hit the lotto, kid.* Diego looks at him and they share a laugh while they resume their work. Before they finish up, Gabe looks across the street for their next prospective customer. His stomach growls and he acknowledges it with a proposition to his boys. *How about Nathan's for lunch? I kinda want some hot dogs with onions.* Shelly hears this and reminds Alby that he promised that they would get a pie, a pizza. He didn't mean to interrupt the group's pace. *Oh yea, a pie sounds good too. No problem, just keep working...*He continues to shovel fiercely as he gives an approving nod to his coworkers. Since they are in the middle of a residential neighborhood that they are unfamiliar with, they decide rather than waste time looking for a place to get pizza nearby, they will just jump on the train, go back to a more familiar neighborhood, and eat lunch and then return. They also know where they can get some good pizza at reasonable prices at a joint called *La Splendita*. They figure a pizza may be a little too pricey around here.

Giles Peterson- "Sandstorm"

Inexplicably, the image of that old lady waiting on Gabe is front and center in his mind. He recalls how his mother would be in the living room after she gave his sisters a bath. She would meticulously do their hair, not being satisfied with just giving them a ponytail. She would work meticulously for hours saying how her babies were going to look so good for school. She took immaculate care of her hair herself, until that day where she fell victim to the rock. After that, she never took care of her locks like she used to. As Gabe tosses a pile of snow onto the area where he assumes may be grass, he looks at the colossal house in front of him and ponders if he had lived in such a home, perhaps his mother would never have left and became hooked on drugs. If he had a magic crystal ball, however, it would likely tell him that that would not have made much of a difference at all.

Waking the few daydreamers, the front door opens and Mr. Taylor appears front and center. Immediately, he pays Gabe, counting the money out loud, and walks down the cleanly shoveled driveway before he opens the door to his car. Gabe's eyes get large, because Mr. Taylor gave him an additional twelve dollars.

Mr. Taylor-*That's a great job, guys; I gotta go but make sure you finish up before you leave, alright?* Collectively, the guys all nod. He stares at the bicycle leaning against the garage and his blood pressure rises while he shakes his head and looks at himself in the rear view mirror. One last time, he checks on his tie; it is flawless. Mr. Taylor smiles to nobody in particular and begins to feel very good about himself and self-assured; then again, most bullies usually feel good about themselves after they have just bullied someone. He backs out the parking spot since there is an enormous pile of snow in front of the car, waves to the guys with a fake smile, puts the car in drive and is gone. Meanwhile, inside, Mrs. Taylor is reassuring her son that everything is going to be okay while she fixes her face and clears the kitchen table. Her son is in the corner talking out loud. His mother asks who he is talking to and he replies, *Blazer.* She soothes her son and reinforces his imaginary friend that brings him comfort and solace. Blazer always shows up when Mr. Taylor is on a rampage.

As the guys wrap things up, they wait for Shelly to finish the stoop and give the house a final once over.

<u>Gabe</u>-*Looks good to me.* He looks to Diego for approval, who in turn looks to Brixx. Together they all agree it is a fine job. *Okay, Shelly, you did a great job, let's go to the next house.* Shelly looks up to his brother who smiles and waves him over. Inside, however, Mrs. Taylor puts some ice on her son's head because there is now a lump. She is currently glad school has been cancelled today and thinks aloud how she would have explained this one to the school, even though the people where she is dropping her son off may have some concerns. Suspicions are certainly going to rise pretty soon like a phoenix from its ashes. As they prepare to leave, she has a thought that is not a novel one: to pack up all their belongings and get as far away from this monster as they possibly can. She threatened this once and needless to say, he was not very happy; he emphatically stated if she ever did, he would find her and put her body in the East River, in segments. As she impulsively contemplates her options, she cannot muster up the courage to put it into action; she never does. Looking in the rear-view mirror, she curses herself for ever even considering it. Remarkably, she convinces herself that he is a good man, a good provider, a good husband and a good father. What would they do without him? Who would want a 43 year old single mother like her? Her looks have dwindled, her brain is frazzled, and her esteem has not been seen since the last administration. This is an image that Mr. Taylor has imprinted in her mind hundreds of times. He would always challenge her to leave and then tell her that nobody would want her at this stage of her life. She slides in behind the steering wheel, wipes the last teardrop from her cheek, forces a smile on her face and asks her son if he has everything he needs. Holding the ice pack against his skull, he nods as they both sniffle safely in the vehicle. With Blazer beside him, he feels out of harm's way and not so alone. For a moment she thinks of staying home with her son today and giving them both a much needed day off. On second thought, she changes her mind, as she often does, and turns the key in the ignition.

Snowgoons- "I Walk Alone"

The little boy begins shouting Blazer's name and striking out, taking his frustration out on his imaginary friend. His mother looks at him through the rear view mirror and shakes her head. She attempts to calm him down but she is unable. In her mind, she wonders what kind of lingering effect all this is going to have on her only son.

Alone
In the darkness
A terrified child
In an impenetrable box
Scared to leave
Free from insanity
Safely tucked away
Not coming out
Of my bunker
Until the war is over
No more bombs
No more violence
The enemy gone

Once the screams subside
A false calmness takes over
And I ponder my options
I retreat slowly
Reluctantly
Cautiously
Peripheral vision on
Every sense keen
Slowly creeping around the corner
I hear a muffled woman
She is terrified
She is crying

D.G. Mago

She is hurt
She is my mother
I go to her
Console her
She begs me to leave her
Return to safety
Because the enemy is returning
I hear him drawing closer
I freeze
Prepared to stand and fight
He reveals an evil grin
He inches closer
Speaking a foreign tongue
Reeking of liquor
Striking my mother with a closed hand
Kicking me in the ribs
I feel sharp pain
I begin to cry
I run to my shelter
And close the door behind me
Petrified
Hoping he doesn't find me
Waiting for the attack to end
I hear screams and crashes
I ignore the yells
My mother's pleading
Amidst the chaos
Blazer holds me tight

I go back to better days
Without the monster
I dream of barbecues
And football games
Of being held and coddled
The noises grow in decibels
I try to drown it out with humming
Blazer sings to me

Closing my eyes
Covering my ears
Sitting perfectly quiet
Holding my legs close to my torso
In the fetal position
Oscillating back and forth
Safely hidden
In my bedroom closet

Day after day
Night after night
Hiding
Never knowing what I might find
When the smoke clears

That tiny space became my haven
My only escape
My world
I sat there many times
Endured many battles
One just like the next
I slept there
I ate there
I played there
It was my world
My only sanctuary that existed
And to this day
Many years after the assaults
A full grown man utterly consumed with both rational and irrational fears
Whenever I am frightened
Or need to retreat
I go to my bedroom
And hide in the closet
A terrified child
Blazer my only ally
Waiting for the enemy to leave
Waiting for the war to end

Ja Rule- "New York"- Instrumental Version

The guys make their way down the driveway and into the street. The sidewalks are too entombed with snow to walk on, so the street becomes the main thoroughfare today. Quickly, the guys knock out three more houses with ease. At the last one, Gabe is getting paid and the price they agreed upon was $25, however, the lady gives him $35 by mistake. Upon noticing this, Drew immediately tells the woman so.

Drew-*You gave us ten dollars too much.*

Woman-*You're right, what an honest young man.* Drew just smiles and Gabe looks at Diego angrily like they just lost out on some money. Gabe reluctantly gives the woman ten dollars back as she thanks them again. As they walk down the stoop and into the street Gabe confronts Drew.

Gabe-*Yo, what was that all about?*

Drew-*What?*

Gabe-*I thought you wanted to make some money.*

Drew-*Yea, but not rip nobody off.* He looks to the others for support.

Diego-*He's right, it was the right thing to do.* Gabe just looks disappointed.

Brixx-*It's just like you wanting to help that old lady out, right, we coulda got more than five bucks but you were trying to help her out, right?* Gabe knows that is not the only reason he wanted to help the old lady but he doesn't want to show his cards, so he just agrees with the guys.

Alby-*Both of yuse are wrong, we need to get paid today, they can afford it! They ain't gonna miss it! All these people got money, look around! Jeez, they wanna spend it.* He looks around and points to the large houses. *Look, they got more than enough. All these people are rich, man, ten, twenty bucks ain't gonna hurt none of 'em. Since when did all of yuse become so damn righteous? Like you fools go to church or somethin'.*

Diego-*And what if someone tried to rip your moms off of ten bucks, huh?* He looks at his friend waiting for an answer. Alby contemplates his answer for a moment. Diego walks up to Gabe, extending his hand. Gabe agrees that it was the right thing to do and reaches for Diego's. He can see that Diego is right and Diego also understands why Gabe wants to help out that old lady but will keep it a secret. Gabe grabs Diego's hand and it disappears in a black hole, swallowed up by Gabe's large paws; it is like putting his hands in a catcher's mitt. Diego takes comfort in Gabe's handshake, overwhelmed by a feeling of safety like a child does when his father grabs his hand before they cross the street. Since Diego has been without a father for quite some time now, Gabe's embrace is the closest he is going to get to that kind of relationship for quite a while. Although his relationship with his grandfather if outstanding, it is his grandfather not his father; nobody can replace that.

Immortal Technique-"Mark of the Beast"

The next three houses they go to they are turned down. As they walk away from the third, the father leaves the house and says goodbye to his family in Spanish.

Father-*Nos vemos.* Cruz stops dead in his tracks and focuses on a fixed point in the snow. Those are the last words he remembers his father saying to him before he left to work, never to return; it means see you later. As the others cross the street, he follows behind from a safe distance, transported to a time when he had both his mother and his father in the home. Cruz and his father were really close. His father was so into soccer and followed his favorite team in Mexico, Cruz Azul; he joked with his son that the family was named after that team. When Cruz went to school one day and made a drawing of the team's logo he felt so proud; he knew his dad was going to love it. He meticulously made sure not to color out of the lines, and then carefully placed it in an envelope to safeguard it from bending. Smiling internally and externally, he walked home hoping nobody would snatch it out of his book bag and ruin it. He remembers walking up the staircase and entering the apartment as he unwrapped the drawing and placed it on the counter in front of his father's photo. He didn't even look for anything to eat that day. Staring at the front door, he waited for his father to come home. However, that day, he simply waited and waited, because his father never did make it home. The devastating feeling he had when he found out his father would not be coming home burned a hole in his stomach like a cigarette into a couch cushion. That burning sensation comes back every time he thinks of him, like right now. That picture is now back in the original envelope, resealed, and under his bed.

Gabe-*Cruz, you dreaming about Veronica again or what? C'mon bro, pick up the pace.* He starts to give Cruz a hard time, unaware his friend is lost in another place and time. Gabe begins to address the others. He makes fun of Cruz's height, because his girlfriend, Veronica, is six inches taller than he, even though Gabe exaggerates and says a foot. *He gotta stand on a desk just to be the same size. Man, she's like six feet tall, she's gonna be playin' in the WNBA if she keeps growing.* He waits for a second until they make eye contact, then turns around and heads up to a beautiful house surrounded by a white picket fence, just like on television. The name on the mailbox reads Gipson.

Tami Chynn- "Hyperventilating"

Don't judge me
I like what I like
Don't call me perverted
Because you have done things even worse
Don't label me
Because we can all be placed in a box

In the roman times
What I am doing was commonplace
It was legal
Just because it is illegal doesn't mean it is wrong
The government just wants to control everything
And leave me with no rights whatsoever
They have brainwashed you into believing I am wrong
That I am sick
Don't believe them
You smoke weed don't you?
You go through red lights don't you?
You have thrown litter on the floor haven't you?
Alright then

They are just so innocent
And pure
Their skin is smooth and unfiltered
Their minds are fresh and uncluttered
Their bodies are clean and unblemished
They are willing participants
Whether I feed them sweets or not
They come looking for me
As much as I look for them

I used to be just like them
Innocent and pure
Until I saw the light
My uncle molested me and had me believing I liked it
And you know what, I think I did
I don't see him as a villain
More a teacher
It is something I had to learn sooner or later
Why not keep it in the family
His idiosyncrasies have now been passed on to me

I like to teach
I am patient and gentle
It only gets rough if they misbehave
And then they must be disciplined
In a way, you can look at me as a professor

It is our little secret
My mother does not know
My ex-wife never knew
The people closest to me have no idea who I really am
What I really like
What turns me on
And what I am capable of

Anyway, what goes on in the privacy of my home
Is only my business
Tend to your worries and your problems
Because I know you have them
It is just much simpler for you to focus on me
That way you don't have to face the fallacies in your families and relationships
So before you want to come in my home and make changes
Make sure your home is uncluttered and free of skeletons
And leave me be
For I have new friends to meet
And new pupils to groom

Gnarls Barkley- "Monster"

Inside the welcoming house, Mr. Gipson is attentively working on the computer when the doorbell rings. He puts the computer in stand-by mode and walks to the front door. Upon opening the door, he sees five young boys and greets them warmly with a huge smile; he pays no attention whatsoever to the young lady in front of him.

Mr. Gipson-*Hello boys, how can I help you?* He is wearing a light blue button down shirt with a heavy maroon sweater over it. Originally, he is from the south and his southern drawl is obvious. For Shelly, it reminds him of his classmate and enamors him.

Gabe-*Would you like your driveway and stoop shoveled today, sir?* Gabe suddenly transforms to the suburban version of himself which is much more approachable and acceptable; he is starting to get good at this. Brixx is also on the stoop, but Mr. Gipson looks right past her like a flight attendant ignoring the people in coach. He looks directly in Gabe's eyes and asks a few questions which are answered with the quickness. After they agree on a price, Mr. Gipson retreats inside the house, but not before chatting the boys up a bit more.

Mr. Gipson-*So, how old are you boys?* The boys respond and feel like they are back in school with all the questioning. After a few moments, he just has one more question. *Would you boys like some hot chocolate?* They all agree that hot chocolate would be great. Brixx is wondering what about her; uh, she would like some hot chocolate too! It is so icy out and the wind has picked up. For that reason alone, hot chocolate would be such a luxury right about now. Just the thought of it has Shelly licking his lips in anticipation. He listens to the way Mr. Gipson pronounces his words and to him it is mesmerizing. Ever since he was a teenager, Mr. Gipson has liked the feel of raw bacon, and always wanted to walk around the streets wearing a mask, a different one every day.

Alby-*What a nice guy! Nobody else offered to make us hot chocolate.*

Drew-*That one lady wouldn't even let me use the bathroom.*

Alby-*Well, you do look like a damn thief today, Drew… and you kinda funky too…* The others agree and chuckle a bit as they get to work. *She probably thought you were gonna leave a deuce in her bathroom!*

Brixx-*I wouldn't trust you in my bathroom either; you know you don't wash your hands after you take a poop! You're just uncivilized!* The guys laugh at Drew. Shelly thinks the group is talking about his older brother and he has two cents to add.

81

<u>Shelly</u>-*She's right, Alby, you don't wash your hands after you poop…and you never spray either.* He looks on innocently as the group gets loud and laughs some more at them both. Alby gives his little brother a dirty look and tries to protect himself like an alleged offender defending himself in court.

After Mr. Gipson begins to make the hot chocolate, he sits back behind his computer and resumes his work. However, it is not really work he is looking at. No rational person would consider it work. Rather, he is looking at some web sites on naked underage boys; he is looking at kiddy porn. He puts his hand down his pants, touches himself, and flips through pages and pages of naked children on the screen.

Mr. Gipson was not only sexually abused himself like many pedophiles, but the issue lies even deeper. As a child, he was picked on constantly, humiliated, tormented and ridiculed by other children. In adolescence, nothing changed and the trend continued; he was beaten and tormented. This abuse led to him longing for legitimate feelings of power. As a result, in his adulthood, he desperately sought ways to regain that power and control. The way he did that was at the expense of those physically weaker than he. Most people believe pedophilia is a sexual crime; actually, it is a crime of power and control. Even though the methods used may be sexual in nature, the root is always power and control. This man never had neither power nor control at his disposal; he was a victim. He had a victim's mentality all his life until he found a way to victimize others. It gave him that feeling of dominion and subjection that he lacked and yearned for all his childhood and adulthood.

Shelly can't stop talking about the hot chocolate and Mr. Gipson's accent while he is feverishly working on the stoop which has iced up. Gabe and Brixx are busy talking to a neighbor who has called them over and arranged to have her house shoveled immediately after they are done at Mr. Gipson's house.

<u>Diego</u>-He looks over at his partners and yells. *Yo, that's another 30 bucks as soon as we finish this one, so let's hump it and get paid.*

<u>Cruz</u>-*After that one, it's lunch time boys! Yabba dabba doo!* He imitates Fred Flintstone at quitting time. Upon hearing the word *lunch*, Shelly picks his head up yet again to remind his brother that he promised him pizza.

At this point, Mr. Gipson has grown bored with the images on his personal computer, and is now spying on the boys outside, all the while touching himself. Oblivious to being watched, the boys continue working. The kettle boiling and whistling startles him and interrupts Mr. Gipson's enjoyment for the moment, as he retires into the kitchen to get the mugs ready. He reaches into the cabinet for marshmallows and begins talking to himself in an often rehearsed soft voice.

Reks- "Money and Power"

Meanwhile, Shelly is having difficulty with the stoop because portions of it have iced over and he tells the others so. Alby joins him on the stoop to show him how to get the ice up more efficiently. Suddenly, the door opens, startling Alby, and there stands the aforementioned Mr. Gipson who has a tray full of mugs of hot chocolate with marshmallows floating on top. He calls the boys over who excitedly run over like it is chow time in an old western.

Drew-*Thanks mister, mmm marshmallows!* They all thank him as he smiles, taking pleasure in providing the boys with a sweet treat, and hoping that later they can return the favor. Brixx gets her mug last and is now oblivious to the fact that he is mingling exclusively with the boys. She watches the marshmallows float on top of the steamy drink like vacationers in the pool at an all-inclusive resort in Cancun. Alby snaps his fingers right in front of her face to wake her up. Once her eyes focus, she hits him with the back of her hand which forces him to take a few steps back. Alby chuckles to himself aloud.

Mr. Gipson-*Careful boys, it's awfully hot.* He notices that Shelly has some chocolate running down his face and with his thumb wipes the chocolate away. *I have some delicious cookies that would go so perfect with this; I'll be right back.* He winks at the boys then excuses himself.

Diego-*Nice guy, huh?* They all concur. Once inside, Mr. Gipson immediately puts that same thumb in his mouth and savors the taste; meticulously, he massages his gums with that finger. He then walks into the kitchen to retrieve some cookies. When he returns outside with a round metal tin filled with all different types of cookies, he has more questions for the boys. Gabe quickly finishes his drink, and encourages the others to do the same. He reminds them that there is a lot of work to be done.

Gabe-*Remember, we got a lot of houses to hit! We can't be dilly-dallying.* He likes that word because his father always uses it. As he walks down the stoop, he grabs his shovel as the others hurry to resume their work. The impromptu reverberation of the metal scraping against the concrete makes Mr. Gipson shudder. He makes his way back inside and lurks behind the curtain, peering with inappropriate thoughts at the boys. Diego continues to smack his lips over and over. Cruz savors the taste on the back of his tongue one last time.

<u>Diego</u>-*Dam, those are some good ass cookies!*

<u>Cruz</u>-*I know, right, fancy too.*

<u>Drew</u>-*Yea, much better than those sorry ass Hydrox cookies we're used to!*

<u>Gabe</u>-*I know that's right.* He says it without looking up from the ground. Quickly, he motions with his head for the others to get back to work. Soon enough, Gabe and Cruz have finished their portion and rather than help the others, they decide to go get started on the neighbor's house; time is moving fast and hunger has crept up on the boys like a demonic entity on an unsuspecting teenage babysitter. Gabe looks the house over and plans his course of action with Cruz. The owner, Mrs. Mapes stated that they won't have to do the driveway because her car is in the street. When she said won't it sounded like *woont* which made Cruz laugh out loud; Gabe hit him in the back with his glove.

<u>Gabe</u>-*Yo, Diego, make sure the house looks good before you guys come over, woont you?* Diego gives him a nod without looking up, focusing on the job at hand. Only Cruz and Gabe got that joke and they laugh to themselves. Ten minutes later, it appears it is all done except for the stoop, which still has patches of ice on it. Alby instructs his little brother to finish the stoop then come next door to help with Mrs. Mapes. Mr. Gipson, upon seeing Shelly all by himself on the stoop, waits a few moments and then opens the door and engages Shelly in conversation.

<u>Mr. Gipson</u>-*Would you like some more yummy hot chocolate and cream cookies?*

<u>Shelly</u>-*Yes…*He looks in the man's eyes not noticing anything evil or dirty. All he sees is the color blue. Only a trained eye would notice beyond the ocean blue, and see a contortion of webs and mazes, a vortex of disgusting ulcers, cankers, and cancers. Shelly gazes undisturbed while his mind focuses on the delectable aftertaste. The sound of Mr. Gipson's voice attracts Shelly like a hummingbird to sugar water.

<u>Mr. Gipson</u>-*Well, come on inside, it's way too cold out here.* He opens the door wider and motions for Shelly to enter, however, Shelly is reluctant. Mr. Gipson's soothing voice is not enough to entice Shelly indoors. His responsibility to his brother suddenly takes precedence.

<u>Shelly</u>-*Alby told me to finish the stoop and if I don't, he won't buy me pizza for lunch…I want a pie.* Immediately he looks to the ground and begins shoveling with more force trying to get all the ice up.

<u>Mr. Gipson</u>-*Oh, I understand completely.* After you finish, then you can come inside for some more hot chocolate. Shelly shakes his head up and down, snot now forcing its way out of his nose and down his face. Mr. Gipson waits patently with the door wide open; heat escapes the home like a cat locked up in the house all day. Becoming anxious, he looks to the left and then the right and sees no neighbors or

anybody in his sight, except for frail-looking and innocent Shelly, who straightens up and inspects the stoop from the first step to the last. *That looks great.* He leads with his head for Shelly to enter. Shelly's eye grow larger just with the idea of some more marshmallows, as he wipes his nose with the back of his forearm and takes his first step into the house. Mr. Gipson's mouth salivates as well, but his for different reasons. Once Shelly takes his second step inside, Mr. Gipson is aroused and can barely contain his excitement. He opens the door a bit wider to let Shelly pass. He then leans in so Shelly has to make contact with him, bends over to get a smell of his prey, and quickly shuts the door behind him. At this moment, Alby is cutting across the lawn and sees the door shut with Shelly inside the house. First, he inspects the stoop which looks pretty good, and then he walks up the set of steps two steps at a time. Shelly is poured another mug of hot chocolate and an entire plate of cookies is placed in front of him. He grabs two cookies at a time and looks at Mr. Gipson who has his eyes peeled on Shelly; he reaches out and places the back of his hand against Shelly's cheek as he caresses it back and forth. Shelly pays it no mind as he focuses on the goodies he has before him, just like Mr. Gipson has planned it. Suddenly, there is a knock on the door and Mr. Gipson just ignores it. Once again, there is a knock at the door, this time more forceful. Mr. Gipson walks into the living room, peers out from behind the curtain and sees Alby waiting on the stoop with his hands in his pockets. Unsure of what to do, he just waits and watches. One last time, Alby knocks on the door, but this time louder and longer. Finally, the door opens and Mr. Gipson has a huge grin on his face and invites Alby in to get out from the cold, offering him some more treats. He briefly thinks of the savory butter cookies from Denmark, then catches himself and realizes his priorities

Alby-*No thanks, I just think I should get my brother because we got a lot of work to do today and we're in kinda a rush.* Mr. Gipson wonders if Alby is on to him or genuinely has no idea what he had in store for his little brother. He stares at Alby for a moment attempting to read his thoughts before he is interrupted by Shelly who comes skipping to the door. Alby just assumed his brother used the bathroom and reminds him that the group is doing one more house before they break for lunch.

Shelly-*Alby, I had more hot chocolate! Look at the stoop; I did a good job, right?* Swaying back and forth, he stares at his brother waiting impatiently for some form of approval.

Alby-*Yea, you did a real good, Shelly, now let's get moving next door.* Reluctantly, Mr. Gipson allows the boys to leave and instructs them that if it snows again tonight to please return tomorrow to shovel his driveway yet again. The boys agree and say goodbye, as he watches them walk away, already plotting his next move. *He sure is a nice guy, huh?* His brother nods in total agreement. Nobody realized the monster that lurks behind those burgundy curtains, and Mr. Gipson's secret is safe for yet another wintery day. Quickly they walk next door and rejoin their friends who are busy shoveling snow.

<u>Drew</u>-*Bout time! D'ya bring some of those bangin' cookies?* They all just laugh and begin to talk about the prospect of having to return to school tomorrow.

Si*Se- "Mariposa en Havana"

Brixx stretches her legs and neck. She has become a bit sore from all the physical labor. However, she has not complained or even grimaced all day; she wouldn't give the boys the satisfaction even if her back was breaking or her fingers were bleeding. She glances across the street and sees some kid making a snowman. Upon further examination, she notices it is a little girl, and she is constructing the snow model with what appears to be her father. Her nose begins to run, and her father takes out a tissue and wipes it for her. The little girl smiles at her father and gives him a hug. He pats her on the head gently and glides gracefully to pick up a huge mound of snow.

Brixx is immediately transformed back in time to a place where her father was actually present and involved. She recalls how he would call her his little princess and be so interested in everything she had to say, no matter how trivial or childish. She could not wait to get home from school to jump on his lap and tell him what she had learned that day in school or what projects she had made in her class. Any time she would get a certificate or commendation, she would wrap it tightly, to ensure absolutely nothing would mark or stain her prized possession on her long journey home from school. She would drool with anticipation of sharing it with her father, who would shower her with positive reinforcement and affection. Wow, does she long for those days all of a sudden with a vengeance. Once again, she reaches in her back pocket and removes her crumpled drawing. She always tells people who ask about her father that she does not care anymore. *Whatever* is her response more often than not when people pursue the subject. She acts nonchalant and apathetic about his disappearing act and nonexistence in her and her mother's life now. However, secretly, she misses him deeply. This display across the street has ushered something up in her that is traveling like a roller coaster falling downhill then upward for a 360 degree turn; it is her breakfast. Suddenly, her stomach feels queasy and she has to bend over. Her hair falls from under her crooked hat. Nausea overtakes her for a brief moment before she finds the strength to push it down like a garbage man standing over an overfilled trash can after the holidays. Gabe notices this and shouts if she is okay. She waves him off while she breathes deeply, shoving her drawing back in her jeans without much care. She catches her breath, tucks her hair back under her wool hat, and looks one final time across the street. She inhales through her nose and exhales through her mouth, as the smoke rises past her teary eyes. The little girl across the street laughs and screams with joy as her father lifts her to put a carrot in the place where a nose should be. Together they stand back and admire the gift they have just created for anyone who is lucky enough to pass by that day. Brixx just shrugs her shoulders and looks away before it hurts too much. Nausea now turns to craving which quickly transforms into indignation. She digs in the ground with her shovel with such force that it strikes the sidewalk, and she feels the vibration go from her hand all the way up her arm into her neck. She cracks her neck and with that motion, strikes it all from her memory like a stroke of an eraser on a chalkboard. That is how in control of her feelings she is, or so she believes. She used to be loved like that, but to remember ancient times and not have it, hurts her to the core. Out of her peripheral vision, the snowman appears to be mocking her; she thinks to herself and stares back. *What are you smiling at?* Her breathing gets heavier as she begins to be consumed with violent thoughts. The snowman seems to be rubbernecking and will not look away. His grin turns wider and now he appears to be smirking sarcastically directly at her. For a brief moment, she thinks she sees him point and chuckle at her as in a pseudo mockumentary. As a result, before she leaves that street, she promises herself one thing. That snowman across the street, grinning from ear to ear is going to be decapitated before this day is done. Believe that!

Ocho- "Undress My Mind"

Don't look at me like that
I didn't do anything
Especially to you
I've never even met you
I'm just minding my own business
I'm no threat to you
I'm no threat to anyone
C'mon, I have a carrot as a nose
Two pieces of charcoal as eyes
Chunks of gravel comprise my smile
All I'm wearing is a hat and scarf
I don't even have snow balls
How can I be a threat?

I know my life expectancy is short
But I at least thought I had until winter's end
Not just a few hours
Why are you so hostile?
Did this family do you wrong?
I don't see how that is possible
They are a loving family
They treat each other with respect
They spend quality time together
Perhaps you are mistaken

Oh, I get it
You are not angry at them
You are jealous of them
Because your family is not invested like that
They are fractured like the dish you dropped
The moment you discovered your dad was never coming back
Hey, that's not my fault

I'm an innocent bystander
I'm just another Christmas ornament
I was created with love
I'm supposed to represent innocence and happiness
If you smite me down
It's like destroying a sandcastle
Or popping a birthday balloon
It won't make you feel any better
Your resentment will still remain and linger
It will fester like an untreated wound
Which is exactly what you have
Please I can help you
I give people joy
I make passersby smile
I bring people together
I help people focus on how fortunate they truly are
There is still time for you
More time than I have
Because even in these fleeting moments
I can't afford to take things for granted
You have an eternity
The rest of your life
So perhaps you should focus on what you do have
As opposed to what is missing
Because even if you gather up all the pieces of that
broken dish and glue them back together
Making that dish whole
I'm sorry to say
Your dad aint coming home
So get over it
And leave me alone

Brixx thinks about that dish that slipped out of her slippery grip that day, and all again is consumed with rage. Once again she stares at the snowman with his snide grin. Is he mocking her? Is he trying to get into her head? This sign of disrespect will not go unpunished. She resumes her work with voracity as Diego and Drew see how violently she is throwing piles of snow. Alby sees this and can't be out worked by a girl, so he begins working extra hard. This attitude becomes contagious and the entire group is working at an Olympic pace. Mrs. Mapes sees this and is amazed; she reminds herself to make sure she gets these kids phone number because they are working like it is going out of style.

<u>Mrs. Mapes</u>-*You kids are doing a wonderful job, I woont forget this and I'm going to tell all my neighbors how terrific you are.* She shouts to the group to ensure her car is shoveled out properly and please not to forget.

<u>Cruz</u>-*Don't worry, we woont!* By now the whole group got the joke and they laugh it up in the cold; everyone that is with the exception of Brixx.

Public Enemy- "Can't Trust It"

Once they finish the neighbor's house, they contemplate their next move: keep working vs. lunch; that is a huge dilemma when dealing with teenagers. Before she leaves, however, Brixx stares at the snowman who is taunting her at this current moment. She lifts her shovel like Spartacus about to battle a roman soldier, when Gabe grabs her arm and escorts her in the right direction. Unanimously, lunch has won out as they rapidly make their way to the train station.

Gabe-*This way Brixx, you drunk or something?* He asks her without knowing what is going on in her heart. The anger and sorrow mix together until she punches Gabe in the arm. Even with all his winter gear on, it pierces through the armor and makes him grimace. *Dam, girl, you hit like a dude!*

They coincidentally pass a local pizza parlor and the aroma is overpowering. Hunger is paramount right now and together they figure instead of wasting time on the train they can eat here then resume working much faster; the prices are reasonable and the smells are undeniable; once they got a whiff of this joint, it was a done deal. The name of the place is Snoiglini's Pizza and Pasta. Shelly hears the change of plans and is discouraged. He wanted to eat at the local pizza parlor he is familiar with because he loves it there. His brother instructs him that the pizza here is even better and with that, he quickly changes his tune. They all agree and enter, order two large pies, one with extra cheese the other with pepperoni and sausage, and two pitchers of soda, one grape the other root beer. As they walk to a nearby booth by the window, Drew bumps into a large boy by mistake, maybe 17 years old; this boy resembles Harry Potter with the same type of glasses, but much bigger and wider. The arrogant adolescent looks furious and pushes Drew into the wall as some expletives fly. Drew is caught totally off guard.

Boy-*Watch where you're goin asshole!* He stares at Drew, not knowing that he is far from alone. In a flash, Gabe intervenes and gets directly in the boy's face; they are about the same height, but Gabe is giving up about 20 pounds to his older opponent. The boy is used to being brave when he towers over someone, but now that someone is almost the same size, that changes everything. In addition, the look in Gabe's eyes is something this boy has never seen, and it is indeed frightening. Brixx watches the exchange and would love to get her hands dirty; her anger is still boiling over from that sorry ass condescending snowman that she can not get out of her head. She steps up to the plate, but Diego grabs her by the shoulders, letting her know that the situation is well under hand. Brixx would not mind being the enforcer, the goon, if you will on this day, but she realizes that Gabe may get offended if she steps in as well. She doesn't want to overstep any boundaries right now since today is a critical time which can determine her alliance with the guys from this day forward.

Gabe-*Whoa, slow down, why don't you open your eyes, and clean those dirty ass glasses, Harry Potter…*He states it with confidence appearing hopeful to get into an altercation. Drew attempts to get back in the mix. After all, it is his affair, and he is not scared; however, Gabe won't allow him. *What?* Gabe raises his hands in the air and in some unwritten code this means he is asking the boy if he wants to continue this in a physical manner. The boy freezes and is intimidated by his much thinner yet brazen opponent. *You might run shit over here in this corny town, but I ain't from here, son…if you wanna step into the ring…*He inquires now hoping the boy will take him up on it…*I ain't beat nobody in a minute, it's way overdue, son.* Actually, it was just yesterday. *Don't worry; I'll make it quick, like play station…*The teenager looks Gabe in the eye but only for an instant before looking away, afraid to maintain eye contact showing his weakness. Gabe can tell he is contemplating his next move; what will it be, flight or fight? *Come strong or don't come at all.* He states it with an undeniable conviction. Gabe begins to speak slower and pronounces each syllable meticulously. *Want some…get some.* Gabe continues to leer at his opponent, waiting for any indication that he has accepted the challenge. Instead, the nervous boy shakes his head and walks away mumbling to himself. That glare of angst and determination in Gabe's eyes translates into **crazy** for this boy and he wants no part of it. *Better go back to that busted castle Potter, before I turn you into a toad!* The others begin to laugh as Gabe watches the boy exit the restaurant, and when they make eye contact through the glass window, he points a finger at him and fires an imaginary bullet at him. The boy exhales with relief as he begins to trot. As soon as he is out of view; the trot turns into a dash and before long he is at full speed and gone. Brixx admires the way Gabe handled that and figured if it was her, she would probably have just belted the boy in the mouth. *Don't think I forgot about you though…*She deliberates internally about that patronizing snowman with that demeaning grin on his face.

Drew-*I coulda handled that.* He states with confidence, hoping the others didn't think he was afraid.

Gabe-*I know, but. . .* Shelly interrupts and wants his pizza **now**. Actually, Drew was hoping he'd get a chance to fight someone. That way he could relay it back to his older brother who is gang banging, since that is the only way he can possibly get some positive reinforcement from him these days. He used to be able to bring home an **A** from school and get a slap on the back, but now it must be some shady or delinquent act from the streets to get his brother's attention.

Gabe was also hoping to get a crack at another victory, because he has plenty of displaced anger that has gone unresolved concerning his mother. Harry Potter would have been just another statistic that was in the wrong place at the wrong time, another notch in the belt like that of a savvy gunslinger. Subconsciously, Gabe is actually hoping for a loss; that way he could reevaluate his anger control and perhaps do something positive about it. Until then, however, he believes will just be bouncing from one fight to the next, playing out all the rage he has concerning his mother. Displaced and unresolved anger will be a constant theme in these boys' lives for quite a while; it will repetitively and habitually return like a well oiled revolving door in a five star hotel.

Once they do actually take a seat, they go over what just happened all over again. When the pizza is ready, Cruz and Brixx go and bring the food to a table. Shelly slides in first and makes sure Alby sits beside him. Brixx sits across from him so she can look out the window. Shelly is in heaven as Alby must constantly instruct him over and over to blow on the pizza because the cheese is scorching. Once he takes a bite, the cheese slides off the slice and rips right into his bottom lip; he quickly drops it down on his paper plate, puts a napkin to his burning lip, and finally waits patiently for the food to cool. The others laugh at him; *a beginner* they verbalize aloud. Looking like a puppy who knows he did wrong, Shelly dabs his lip with the napkin as his eyes begin to water up. Holding back the tears, he wants to cry but his hunger overrides anything else at the moment. All the while, he is indeed concentrating on sinking his teeth into the slice directly in front of him. The grease from the pizza makes the paper plate as useless as a screen in a submarine. Cruz gets up and walks to the counter to politely ask for more paper plates and practice his vocabulary in the process.

Swollen members- "Aggression"

There is a television in the corner of the restaurant, and the local news is on. A man has been arrested and is filmed being put in the squad car in handcuffs. Alby looks away and out the window, recalling the day his father was arrested. He was coming home from school, and he and his friends saw two police cars in front of their housing project. That is not anything new; that is a normal scene almost on a daily basis there. However, this day, the person leaning against the back of the cruiser in handcuffs was Alby's father. He tossed his book bag off of his shoulders and ran to the car as fast as he could. When he was within talking distance, out of breath, he loudly asked where they were taking his father. Nobody answered him, so he repeated it only this time louder. One police officer told him to calm down and took him aside. With tears in his eyes, he listened and knew that that moment would be the last he would see his father for a long time. Even at that age, he understood his father was going away and would not reappear until many Christmases would pass. He does not know why, but that is precisely what he thought about. *How many Christmases will pass before I see my dad again?* The answer up until this point is now four. He looks at Shelly who has no idea what he is thinking and wonders if he even remembers him. Once again, he asks himself that question that haunts him. *How many more Christmases will now pass before I see my dad?* The news shifts to the weather report as the kids listen in, hoping for nothing but more snow. Alby reminisces more about his departed father. He fondly recalls when he was much smaller, how he would enjoy his father's laughter. His laugh was something between a guffaw and a snort; it made the most hilarious sound. No matter what he laughed about, it became funny to Alby, because of his father's laughter. It was loud and course, and always drew attention. Even if he was not in the room, he could even have his bedroom door closed, and if he heard that giggling, it would make him delirious with laughter himself. Whenever he was down or sad, his father would always know what would cheer him up: a dose of dad's laughter. He would sneak up behind him and start tickling him. Then when Alby would begin to laugh, his father would join in, and before long they would both be in stitches, side by side, cracking-up out loud. What he wouldn't give to hear that jubilation now. Every now and then, he looks behind him wondering if his dad is sneaking up behind him to tickle him. The smile on his face slowly dissipates as he sternly instructs his brother, once again, to blow on the pizza slice before he takes a bite.

The boys, and Brixx, eat their lunch joking and clowning, and planning the rest of their day, including how much money they can possibly earn. By now, Brixx has calmed down and with food in her stomach, she relaxes. After approximately thirty minutes, Diego suggests that they leave in ten minutes, to return to their business and everyone rigorously agrees.

Alby-*Well, did you get enough pizza? Was it good?* Talking to his brother, Shelly, who simply nods his head over and over and tells Alby he now wants to go home. Gabe quickly looks at Alby who instructs his brother. *Listen, you said you wanted to come…I got you pizza, now you have to work the rest of the day, or else I'm gonna take you home and leave you there all by yourself for the rest of the day!* Shelly quickly agrees to resume his work, because to be left alone by himself is too terrifying a thought. The others look relieved to hear that their posse would not be split up today, or, more paramount, their earning potential. Alby takes Shelly into the bathroom to make sure he uses it and washes his hands good; he doesn't want any more complaining or whining today. Once they put their winter coats on, they grab their respective shovels, and head out into the cold, where the temperature has dropped a couple of degrees. The wind whips Brixx in the back of the neck and she quickly wraps her scarf to blanket the uncovered area. Gabe notices her bare neck for a brief second, and stares longer than he wants to. He then proceeds to pack some snow together hurriedly and puts it under Brixx's scarf. She screeches like a girl which surprises all the guys. She gathers herself and chases Gabe around the corner. The others just laugh and then turn the corner in hot pursuit.

Chambao- "Lo Mejor Para Ti"

I grew up in a small town in the Midwest
A long ways from here
I am without any friends or family
I did that deliberately because I have been betrayed by both friends and family
I choose to be alone
I grew up on a commune
Everything was organic and natural
Fruits and vegetables were forced down my throat
So you can imagine how I feel about them today
I didn't have my first sugary cereal until I was 12
And that was only because I snuck it without anyone's knowledge
My parents fought all the time
In front of my siblings and I
After years of discourse, they finally and thankfully divorced
And sent us to live with our uncle
He was abusive to my sister and me
After years of trauma and scars
We were put into foster care
The baton was passed like it was a long distance relay race
Where the abuse continued by our foster father
He threatened me into silence
I was coerced to internalize the pain
Although I never ran away
I thought about it hundreds of times
Emotionally, I ran away every day
And every night
So you can see I never left home
In actuality, home left me!
And that hurt so much
And it still does
Yet and still, I never self-medicated

If it wasn't natural, it wasn't for me
It was ingrained in my skull like Lincoln's face in a penny
Nobody was more opposed to medicine, the pharmaceuticals, and drugs than I
But then came the accident
That left me miserable and wreathing in excruciating pain
For a brief while, I was resistant and strong
But the pain grew consistently
Like smoldering fire from a single flame
Pain became chronic and truly unbearable
So I broke down and got a prescription
And sure enough the pain subsided
All the pain
The physical and the emotional
But only briefly
Before I needed more and more
To ease the discomfort

Simply by mistake, I looked in the mirror one day
And noticed a stranger looking back
Someone who **needed** something
And that is something I always prided myself on
I could never count on anyone
When I did, they would just betray me in horrific ways
So it was just me
And now I don't even have that
It's such a pity because the pain has gotten much worse
As a result, I need to take more
And so the cycle continues
Deep down I know I there is a problem
That should really be addressed by a professional
But it hurts so much
All I can think about is alleviating the pain
Hence, I pop a pill and it gets somewhat better
And each time I think this time is the last
But I just fool myself
And I pop another
And another
To be released from this prison of pain

Cheo Feliciano and Pete "El Conde" Rodriguez-"Soneros de Bailadores"

Once they cross the clean and shimmering street, Alby shouts to the others that he wants to shovel the driveway at this yellow house. Drew explains they were supposed to go back to the neighborhood where they were before, since they were getting a lot of business there. Alby is adamant and begs the guys if they could ask the owner to do the yellow house. They don't understand why but agree just to stop his whining; Alby has affection for the color yellow. Unbeknownst to him, his first blanket and teddy bear were the same exact color of this house. Subconsciously, it must bring him comfort and reduce his anxiety. The house in question is a very elaborate house with eclectic décor in the yard and on the porch. The name reads *Henshaw* and of course Alby is the one who has to crack a joke, and poke fun, comparing it to Hee Haw. Gabe and Brixx step to the door together and Gabe steps down so Brixx is alone at the door. She gives him an inquisitive look and he stares her back which without words informs her it's all on her. *Okay*, Brixx thinks as she knocks on the door with a smile on her face. Nobody answers and Gabe tells her to knock louder. She looks back at him in contempt, but complies and knocks harder and longer. They can hear someone rustling around inside and finally the door is unbolted. A woman in her mid forties opens the door meticulously. Brixx politely asks if she would like her driveway shoveled then asks how she pronounces her name. This is something she saw on television doing pretend job interviews; it helps put people at ease. The woman tells her to keep it simple and call her by her first name, Beth. Brixx does her best saleswoman job, and gets the boys another gig, and for good money. Inside the home, music plays. Brixx asks the woman who is the singer and she explains it is Nora Jones. Brixx and Ms. Henshaw engage in a conversation about music, jazz and reggae in particular.

Once Beth closes the door and goes inside, the group begins to work in a tenacious manner. She looks like a very normal woman; attractive with long blonde hair, glasses, and a gracious mixture of nerd and sex appeal. She is educated and holds down a steady job as a medical assistant specializing in urinary issues. Actually, she is too normal. Like many people today, perhaps the majority, she is on prescription medication. Also like many people today, she is abusing those medications and has become addicted. Her drug dealer is not some dirt bag on the side of the road, but rather the drug manufacturer itself, the pharmaceutical corporation. Street dealers and street drugs are slowly and yet rapidly being replaced by a new pusher, the corporations. Crack, coke, and meth are also being pushed aside for more easily accessible prescription medications such as Oxycontin, Percoset, and Vicodin; there is a huge percentage of the population addicted to pain meds.

Gabe and Alby comment on the music heard from in the house. Brixx liked it very much and defends the woman, and her taste in music.

Alby-*Yea, I guess that's good music…if you're in a coma.*

Gabe-*Or maybe it's good music to get you out of a coma.*

Alby-*Yea, if I was in a coma and you guys played that music, I would wake up and curse you fools out… for crying out loud, turn that fuckin music off!!* The guys all laugh and look at Brixx who has her hands folded; a look of discernment brushes over her face as she glares directly at her team members.

Gabe-*If I was on a ventilator and drifting off to the afterlife, I would just go towards the light and away from that music.* They all laugh it up some more.

Alby-*Yea, I don't think there is any appropriate time to play that music…maybe at a funeral…that is pure gobbage*! Brixx punches Alby in the arm. *Ow!* He looks at her and thinks twice about retaliating, but she just stares at him and rolls her eyes. He thinks this is a good time to use the pizza crust in the eyes joke but he notices she has no crust in the corners of her eyes currently. *Dam!*

Brixx-*You smell like gobbage, u idiot!!* She says the word just like he did to make an emphatic point. Diego and Drew watch on with pure deliberation like a pelican watching a fish before it dive-bombs into the ocean after its lunch.

Reks – "What It Is"

The group begins to shovel the snow, while inside, Beth has popped a couple of pills. She sits on the couch and becomes human pudding. She becomes relaxed, very tranquil, and feels no pain. Originally, she had legitimate back pain from a bad car accident. It left her with debilitating torment. Her doctor prescribed some pain pills which eased the pain. However, her tolerance grew and she needed more to ease the pain. Soon enough, she used it not only to alleviate the physical, but also the mental and emotional pain she felt. All she had to do was go to the doctor, describe the pain she was in, and he or she would write a prescription. She would then proceed to the local pharmacy, and get it filled. All legitimate and covered by insurance companies to some extent. It's a genius plan. Just like the local street hustlers who would hand out free drugs to get people hooked on the latest craze and then make a huge profit when they come back begging for more; this scam is on a much larger scale, and it is completely on the up and up.

As if she didn't have enough on her plate, there are some mental health issues that affect her on a daily basis. She suffers from anxiety, depression, and in addition, she is a trichotillomaniac; when she is anxious, she pulls out her own hair. It is an impulse control disorder caused by stress and depression. When the hair is pulled, a sense of relief is felt. One usually pulls one hair at a time and it can last for hours on end. Due to this disorder that some may label as obsessive-compulsive, some people wear wigs. Ms. Henshaw does as well. In the winter, she likes wearing shorts over her sweatpants and only wears men's deodorant. She used to fast for days on end and then torture herself by watching the food channel.

Alby shovels the entire driveway all the way up to the garage, which is a separate structure. He peeks inside and sees a brand new Audi R8 Gt. The retail value hovers just under $200,000. Alby stands with his mouth wide open. He quickly calls Gabe over who also has affection for expensive cars.

<u>Gabe</u>-*Dude, no way! That's top of the line bro! The only thing more expensive is that R8 Gt Spyder. Yo, that is what I'm talking bout! I'm gonna get that one day!* His eyes are huge. Cruz sees his expression and yells to him.

<u>Cruz</u>-*Oy, juevo frito! You okay?* His sister uses that expression a lot and has told the guys that *juevo frito* is Spanish for *fried egg*. At the moment, Gabe's eyes are as

large as two fried eggs. They get into a heated discussion about luxury vs. sports cars. Diego breaks it up and asks if they could get back to work so they can move on to the next home. *You right, but you don't have to have such an obstinate personality my man…*The others look at him in bewilderment, knowing he is just practicing his vocabulary once again.

Ms. Henshaw opens the door and begins talking to Brixx. She asks a few questions but makes no sense at all. She is slurring her words and is relatively incomprehensible to Brixx. Instead of interrupting the lady, Brixx just listens actively and nods her head, not knowing what in the world she is talking about. After a few more question and answer sessions, Ms. Henshaw returns to the warmth of her living room, and pills, while Brixx fills the guys in on the conversation, or lack thereof. Drew asks if the lady was upset with their work and Brixx shakes her head.

Brixx-*I don't know what that lady was talkin about. I couldn't even understand what she was tryin to say. She's nuts!* Gabe wonders if that means she will try to stiff the boys for their hard work. *No, she's gonna pay, the only thing I think I understood was that she only had hundred dollar bills and if we had change.* Alby and Diego look at each other in astonishment.

Alby-*Nuttin but hundreds? Shit, I wish I had that problem; wow…*Everyone nods in agreement before Brixx encourages everyone to hurry up and finish before the crazy lady changes her mind.

Inside, Ms. Henshaw relaxes on the couch in front of her brick fireplace. She calls for her cat to come, but there is no cat residing in the home. Either she has regressed to an early childhood memory, or she is hallucinating. Who knows? She sips on her drink and places two pills ever so gently on her tongue like a mother putting her newborn down for a nap after hours of crying. Slowly she swallows the pills and makes a prolonged and loud *ahhhhh* sound. She stares blankly at the fire in the gas fireplace which is mesmerizing; she does not blink for minutes. Outside, Shelly is working hastily and getting positive reinforcement from Diego, who tells him what a good job he is doing. None of the boys recognize the symptoms of pain medication addiction; it is not commonplace for them, yet. They are rather familiar with the signs of street drug symptoms, but those prescribed by a physician or psychiatrist has barely made its way across the train tracks. However, one of the individuals in the group shoveling snow outside this lady's home will know all too well the symptoms and repercussions of being a pill head or pill popper. By the age of 17, someone here will have some very difficult decisions to make about his or her future and direction in life. It is not clear which direction he or she may choose. Hopefully, the support system in place will be sufficient to help pull that individual out of that pit and put him or her on the path to recovery. All that is clear is that prescription meds will be America's number one addiction very soon. Once again, it will know no color, age, or socioeconomic background. Since the corporations will be the benefactors of such profit, and since corporations have such power and influence in American politics, it is highly doubtful that anything will be done to educate or eradicate. Therefore, welcome to the new millennium.

Afro Cuban All Stars- "Esperanza"

The guys begin talking about the Audi again and how much money it is possibly worth. Drew stares through the glass window of the garage and his breath fogs up the glass. He begins to blink uncontrollably then consciously catches himself and takes a deep breath to gain control. Diego witnesses this and pretends he doesn't. He finishes his portion of the driveway and looks around; seems like they are almost done as Alby and Shelly are finishing up with the stoop. Brixx sees they are just about done so she rings the doorbell and waits for a response. Nothing. She rings the bell again. Still nothing. Gabe runs up the stoop, skipping steps, and knocks on the door. He waits a few moments and knocks even harder. Ms. Henshaw is knocked out, as she releases a snart or two. Her friends and she joke about snarting all the time. A snart is when a person snores and farts simultaneously. She is in a deep sleep and is having a bizarre dream right now. She is dreaming of being in a Broadway theatre sleeping in the balcony as she reclines over two maybe three chairs. Someone with an eye patch is watching her or spying on her. There is a dog with green eyes by her side standing guard. From where she is situated, she can see there is a small man or child riding in a tiny convertible car smoking on a long cigarette or cigar. The pungent smell is overwhelming. He is wearing a beret, a tank top shirt, and has a pair of John Lennon sunglasses masking his eyes. Slung over his shoulder, he has a closed umbrella. There is a Ferris wheel in the background which is turning counter clockwise and at a rapid speed. The creaking of the Ferris wheel is overpowering and is getting louder. On the ground is a genie's lamp with smoke coming out in a spiral motion. The smoke continues upward until it warps into an immense genie also wearing a tank top with polka dots. He has day old stubble, sunglasses, a top hat, and a cross hanging from his neck; his eyes are hidden as well. His hands are wide open and empty. The genie floats around until the entire scene becomes a snow globe and the genie is now on the outside of the globe as well as inside. He appears to be carrying the globe like Atlas, the primordial Titan who held up the celestial spheres. The globe doesn't appear to be heavy, on the contrary, it seems like it is weightless and he bounces it off of his fingertips effortlessly. Joyously, he twirls around in delight. She shouts to the genie how he likes his coffee and he yells back, *creamy*. As she fixes his mug of steaming finca java cafe, the genie bounces the sphere back and forth to himself in a whimsical fashion.

George Shearing- "Caravan"

Gabe whacks at the door with a closed fist one final time before consulting his friends.

Gabe-*Tell me no. . I know she ain't trying to stiff us!* He looks around and contemplates his next move. He knocks again and rings the bell as he peers through the stained glass door panel. He can barely see inside and isn't sure if he can see a person. He knows he doesn't see any movement at all. *C'mon now!* His impatience covers him like a large trench coat on a small child, as he rolls his eyes and looks to the others for suggestions.

Cruz-*Let's just try a couple other domiciles on this street and then come back...* His reasoning is that they don't want to waste too much time since there are other prospective customers on this street. They all hesitantly agree and Gabe grabs the hand rail and walks down the stoop resentfully. He rapidly whirls around thinking he heard something but no, not a thing. They go next door and are turned down. They go across the street and nobody answers the door. At the next house the person is attempting to talk the kids down. The name on the door is Celerin. Alby gets frustrated with all the haggling and just can't contain himself any longer.

Alby-*What kind of name is Celerin? It sounds like celery...Where are you from anyway?* Alby apparently is tired or hungry and has just blown a sale for the group. Brixx gives him a shove and that starts the bickering on the stoop of a complete stranger. Mr. Celerin slams the door and will not be hiring the guys today.

Brixx-*Man, you stupid!* Alby looks at her and calls her stupid. She can tell he is loading up and about to come out with a joke when she beats him to the punch. *Man, you so stupid, you went to the beach and found some seaweed and decided to smoke it thinking you could get high!* Gabe and Diego are leaning on each other as their laughter makes them weak. Alby looks on with his mouth open as Brixx opens up her arms wide motioning for him to come on. Before he can retaliate, Drew refocuses the group on work.

At this point, they decide to head back to Ms. Henshaw and retrieve their money if possible. Brixx and Gabe return to the stoop as the rest wait on the sidewalk staring at the front door like a movie is about to begin. They knock forcefully on the door and it is opened immediately. Beth seems very happy to see the group.

<u>Ms. Henshaw</u>-*I was wondering where you guys went, I looked out and you had disappeared. You guys did a wonderful job, creamy!* She hands Brixx a hundred dollar bill and Brixx in turn gives it to Gabe to make change. Brixx is wondering what she meant by the word *creamy*, but will wait until they get paid to decipher that message. Ms. Henshaw just heard that word in her dream and she is still unsure if this is a dream. Gabe makes change for her and hands it to her. She quickly pushes back another $20 bill and tells the group to come back next time it snows. As she tilts her head, her wig slides to the side, and she is totally unaware of the shift. None of the boys notice this, with the exception of Shelly, because they are staring at the hundred dollar bill. As she straightens up, the wig slides back to the middle and now fits almost perfect. She also was eating some peanuts and fell asleep while she was eating them and they fell out of her mouth onto the couch. While she slept, they stuck to the back of her neck and will stay there for a while. Shelly was the only one who noticed the peanuts stuck on her neck and her wig sliding. Unaware of the huge comic relief they just somehow managed to completely overlook, the rest of the guys, and Brixx, thank her and exit the stoop. Almost immediately, they all begin to talk about the woman. Shelly attempts to tell the guys what he saw, but he is quickly dismissed. Gabe thinks she must be a hippy and Diego thinks she was drunk. The discussion continues as they walk away happy with a little extra pep in their step, and some extra cash in their pockets.

Ghostface Killah- "Motherless Child"

How many hours can I play video games
Be entertained by my state of the art iPad
Or ride my new bicycle
Before I get bored
How many times can I wear my new clothes
Spray myself with name-brand cologne
Or run around with my $200 Nikes
When I have no where to go
How many days can I play with myself
Watch relationships formed with television scripts
Or invent imaginary friends to play with
Before I feel socially isolated

I'll tell you
Not very long

How come I don't have any friends?
How come my parents don't even like me?
How come I am all alone?
These are questions that eat at my vulnerability
Until I internalize each one and feel worthless

I want to go outside and play
Like other kids
I want to go to school and integrate
Like other kids
I want to go far away from here and start over
Like other kids

My father works all the time
He goes out of town every week
When he returns
He always brings me something back

That is expensive and new
Before he leaves again
I just want him to stay with me
Play catch with me
And spend time with me
That's what I really want
If he took a minute to look
At something other than his iPhone
And the NY stock exchange
He would see it in my face

My mother is rarely here
Although she is not employed
She is always getting her nails done
Or having lunch at some fancy restaurant
She always returns smelling or looking like someone else
Before she leaves again

She never cooks me dinner
Or checks my homework
Like other moms
I just want her to stay here with me
And spend some time with me
Play a game with me
Tell me a story
Ask me about my day
About my dreams or goals

That's what I really want
But if she took a minute to notice me
Something, anything other than her appearance and her wants
She would see it in my face

My fish died
And I flushed it down the toilet
My dog was hit by a car
And they have never gotten me another
My best friend is my nanny
And she is 63 years old and from Haiti

The only reason she sticks around is because she is getting a paycheck
My hobbies are playing video games and reading books
I don't even know how to talk to children my age
I don't understand their language
Or customs
It is like I am in a foreign land in my own neighborhood
I have never had a friend before
I don't know how to act
Nobody has ever taught me
Nobody ever teaches me anything
Except my nanny

My dad has not taught me how to be a man
How to command and demand respect
How to be assertive and self-confident
He doesn't even shake my hand
He has not taught me a thing

My mom has not taught me how to love
How to express my feelings
How to approach and treat a lady
She doesn't even hug me
She has not taught me a thing

My nanny is my mother
She is also my father
She is my teacher
She is my only friend
My only confidant
Even if she is faking it
She is the only person that listens to me
The only person that cares about me
The only person I can count on
The only one who is here
Besides me

O'Jays- "For the Love of Money"

When the guys make it around the corner into a new residential neighborhood, they all stop in their tracks for a brief moment. They collectively take in the sight of what looks like to them as Ritchie Rich's house; it is three stories high and has a circular driveway. The boys look at each other, and without saying a word, walk up the winding staircase before stopping at the front door. The name on the welcome mat reads The Mcleans. Alby is fiddling with his teeth and Brixx asks him what he is doing. He tells her and the group that has a piece of pork chop stuck in his teeth. Brixx teases him that it has probably been there for over a month. He pulls and tugs and finally a piece of meat comes out from between his teeth.

Brixx-*That gives new meaning to the phrase pulled pork!* Everyone busts out laughing as Alby stews by himself knowing Brixx just handled him, and with ease. After a few moments, the group finally focuses to the task at hand.

Cruz-*What I wouldn't give to live here!*

Diego-*Would you give up your right leg?*

Drew-*Or your eyes?* Cruz ponders the questions and does not respond until Gabe throws him a curveball.

Gabe-*How about have sex with Mrs. O'Meara?* She is the gym teacher and weighs a good 330 pounds.

Cruz-Without hesitation, he answers that one. *Hell no! I'll go back to the projects in a heartbeat! Now, Diego, I know you'd do it with Mrs. O'Meara…We all know you got a crush on her!*

Gabe-*Yea, son, that's why you're trying to get left back!* They all break out in laughter which is interrupted when the front door opens. The huge wooden door, which is about eight feet high, opens slowly and the boys expect Lurch or some other giant to greet them, however, a small boy playing Play Station Portable appears before them never looking up from his game. Drew takes a few steps towards the boy in amazement.

Drew-*Is that the new Indy 500 game?* The boy nods. *I thought it wasn't even out yet.* The boy explains his father always gets him the newest games before they are available for the public. He then reaches in his pocket of his brand new jeans and pulls out a handful of others to show the guys. Gabe pushes Drew out of the way and is front and center.

Gabe-*Whoa, Pirates of the Caribbean 5! And the Executioner's Vengeance! Dam, son, you got 'em all! No way, he even got Lords of Valor!* The guys look over his shoulder as he plays for his audience and tries extra hard to impress his guests. *What's that one?* He studies it and reads the title out loud. *Massacre at Zombie Hill, they said that wasn't coming out until next year!* The guys commend the boy on his playing skills when he asks them if they want to play. Alby pushes his way past Cruz and Drew to get to the front of the line. Brixx body checks him as he attempts to get past her. Before they get the chance, the housekeeper appears front and center and interrupts play time. She asks them what they want; after they do a convincing enough job to sell their services, she agrees to have them shovel the driveway. The boy appears to be upset that his admirers have suddenly vanished and he has been left alone once again. As the housekeeper closes the door, the boy watches the guys walk down the stoop talking among themselves; he appears to be the hot topic of the day. The guys are very envious of the boy that lives in this monstrosity of a house. Diego and Drew shake their heads in unison.

Drew-*Shit, Mrs. O' Meara ain't really that bad...*He smiles and slyly looks at the others with a raised eyebrow. They are simply shaking their heads and laughing as they maneuver there way down the front staircase.

Shelly-*Alby, did you guys see the peanuts on that lady back there?* He points in the direction they came from and begins to laugh. Alby has no idea what his brother is talking about and looks to the others for assistance. They all shrug their shoulders as Shelly becomes hysterical. *She had the peanuts... stuck to her face and... to her neck...peanuts...*He loses control and laughs so much the others can't help but laugh with him. Now they all are laughing at the top of their lungs. The boy inside hears the laughter and wonders what was so funny. Quickly, he runs to the front window but does not have a good view of all that commotion. *What is so funny?* He thinks to himself as he stumbles rapidly through the living room, past the furniture that he has been trained never to sit on. Walking gently on the forbidden carpet, he glances out the window through the satin drapes, and sees the group of kids just laughing it up; within seconds, it makes him laugh from inside the house. He stares like a starving man looking through a plate glass window at a rotisserie chicken spinning around sluggishly, while it drips with fat and juices. With his face pressed against the window, it fogs up at once and he wipes the window with his sleeve in a counter-clockwise motion to get another view. Together, through the window, they all share a good laugh. Unbeknownst to the guys, they are being observed.

Decidedly, he looks around to make sure the nanny is not within hearing distance, and rushes back to the front door, opens it slowly, and engages his new friends.

<u>Boy</u>-*Hey you guys wanna see something cool?* The guys stop what they are doing and head over to the stoop where the boy has their undivided attention. He begins to hold his breath and starts turning red. They all comment on how red he is getting. He gets redder and redder then close to purple before he stops and collapses on the floor; he almost passes out. The guys pick him up and dust him off asking if he is alright. He begins to see small, gold diamonds and then is back to full consciousness once again. *I can do it again if you like!* They applaud him on how red he got and ask again if he is alright. Alby does want him to entertain the group again. Before he can answer, the door quickly opens behind him and an arm snatches him from popularity yet again. *I was just showing them how red I can get if I want...*The housekeeper scolds him and sends him to his room. Turning red is his talent; it is something he has discovered in his many hours alone in his room. He has learned it is a way to gain attention from others. That is, after all, all he wants at this or any other moment: some attention.

After the boy gains control of himself, he goes to his room on the top floor, puts down his brand new iPhone and looks out the window. With envy, he watches the guys interact; the sound of laughter is overwhelming. Alone, as usual, he puts on his television which is hanging from the wall in his bedroom to temporarily escape from the mundane; it too is state of the art. It is a sixty inch television which is an eighth of an inch wide. On his walls he has collages with pirates and fairies; he has outgrown these prints and is ashamed by them now. When he was younger, the whimsical pictures of fairies and pirates on his walls would scare him at bedtime, and he would crawl under his bed for solace. No longer is he scared of them, but from time to time, he still feels fear and angst, and finds refuge under his bed. There he feels secure, protected, loved. Even though he is alone, the closed quarters and darkness give him a sense of warmth that his mother and father do not provide for him in the least.

Within moments, he gets bored and creeps to the window to watch his audience. Outside, the guys are busy working when Diego notices the boy watching them from his bedroom window. Diego stops shoveling for a moment and looks upwards until their eyes briefly meet. Today has been the most interaction this boy has had with anybody other than his servants in quite a while. The boy deeply wishes he had some friends, someone to play with, to talk with, someone simply to spend time with. Someone hits Diego with a snowball as he whirls around, yet everyone is busy working, covering their tracks very well. When he looks back up to the window, the boy is gone; Diego doesn't think twice about it and resumes working. The boy, however, is consumed with his loneliness as he casually falls into his well of shadows lined with an endless amount of questions. Quickly, he internalizes it all and begins feeling worthless and insecure. These thoughts, however, are neither validated nor discounted by his parents, both of whom are not home and won't be for quite some time. As a result, he is left to search for answers alone, using MTV and HBO as his teachers.

Cruz and Drew begin to discuss what it must be like to live in a house like this, filled with seemingly everything one could ever want.

Diego-*Well, if I lived in a joint like this, I wouldn't invite you fools over, that's for sure.* Gabe begins to laugh and gives Diego the finger. *You fools would have to wipe your feet first, that's real!*

Cruz-*How big you think the T. V. is?* He asks his comrades whose answers range anywhere from 52 inches to 200 inches.

Gabe-*I know one thing, I betcha the fridge ain't never empty! Sometimes when I look in my fridge, I'm blinded by the light, cause there ain't nothin in there but the light bulb.* Everyone laughs but not because it is funny, because it is true and they can all relate to that. *I bet they eat lobster and caviar and shit like that for dinner every day.*

Drew-*You know they ain't eatin no government cheese!* They all shrug their heads in unison. *They got real milk too, not that big ass box of powdered milk.*

Alby-*I hate that shit!* He slams his shovel into the snow and it stands up all by itself. *If I lived here, I'd order pizza every night and have ice cream with butterscotch on it for dessert!* Shelly listens to what the others are saying and looks sad all of a sudden

Shelly-*I wouldn't wanna live here, Alby.*

Alby-*Why not?*

Shelly-*Cause if I lived here, I'd miss my mom.* He looks at the others and his eyes begin to tear up. He sniffs three times and snot begins to run down his nose, barely missing his upper lip.

Alby-*But she'd live here too, dummy.*

Shelly-*No she wouldn't, she wouldn't be here.* The others attempt to explain to Shelly that it would be there home together, yet he doesn't comprehend. On the other hand, perhaps it is the others who do not fully comprehend; the boy who lives there would surely agree with Shelly. Alby just shrugs his shoulders and yanks his shovel out of the snow. He wonders aloud why his brother just doesn't get it, yet it is his brother who has demonstrated an incredible amount of wisdom.

Gabe-*They got a housekeeper too, son. They probably got a butler and a chauffeur!*

Diego-*Shit, I'll be the chauffeur, especially if I'm wheelin in one of them Hummers!* His eyebrows hike up his forehead as he places himself briefly in that fantasy.

Brixx-*The only hummer you gonna get is from that homeless guy we passed who lives in the subway!* The others bust out laughing at Diego. Alby gets a kick out of that and is glad she chose Diego to go after for once. Watching from a careful distance, Alby sees he is going to have his hands full with Brixx today should they go toe to toe.

Descarga Boricua- "Yo No Soy Guapo"

Inside, however, the boy who resides where everyone else desires to live is also in the middle of a sort of fantasy of his own. His, mind you, is much different than the others. His fantasy doesn't focus on where he resides, but with whom, something the others have not thought about with the exception of Shelly. He wishes his mother and father were home much more and when they were, he wishes they were attentive. Not only attentive to their surroundings, but mainly to him. In addition, he wishes he had some friends to play with, talk to, and grow up with. If he could, he would trade places with the guys outside, any of them, in a heartbeat. To be part of a group, to feel loved, to belong, that is all he wants. He could care less about all the **things** he has. They do not bring him comfort, they do not tuck him in at night, they do not tell him *I love you*, and they do not hold his hand, or caress his face, or help him in time of crisis or despair. What he really wants is what the boys outside already have, but take for granted. Conversely, what they really want are the material things that everyone strives so hard to get.

Inside his room, he pulls out a small cardboard box from his pocket and removes some cotton balls that were inside. Out of all his belongings, this is his most cherished one. He begins to stroke the cotton with his thumb and forefinger which makes him feel calm and less anxious. The texture of something soft puts him at ease, always has. He has had that particular box for weeks. If the nanny or his parents find it, they will throw it out and tell him to stop it. He has been doing this for years. However, nobody has either attempted to comprehend why he has the need to touch something soft or done anything to remedy the situation; it has just been dismissed as childish behavior.

The troubled boy has no idea how his parents were raised because they don't engage him in any type of dialogue. His father grew up poor and wanted to give his children much more. He ended up equating love with things, but doesn't realize that time with your child is much more valuable. He must answer his phone if it rings; he can't ever let it go to voicemail. His mother grew up a spoiled brat and has not changed a bit; she has always put her needs and wants before anyone else's. In essence, she does not understand what good parenting requires. Her son is home-schooled, but not by her. The nanny is fully licensed to home teach, which gives the mother a license to go out, play and shop. She constantly walks in the door carrying bags of new things she has bought. Yet one thing that she does not carry whatsoever is a feeling of guilt. She never sits on a toilet seat, even at home. She has immense quads and hamstrings from squatting all these years.

This driveway is taking them a lot longer than most because it is so incredibly huge. Working industriously, the boys engage in some small talk about daily events in the city recently. Cruz likes to be up to date on current events which are encouraged by his family and teachers.

Cruz-*Did you hear about the guy who was trampled to death when he opened the door to Wal-Mart for Christmas shoppers?*

Diego-*That was so messed up, man!*

Drew-*The poor guy was just doing his job and all those crazy people…*The boys get into a discussion about people's greed and their search for wealth and material goods.

Gabe-*Shit, I dunno, if they had a sale on those plasma TV's and some fool was standing in my way, I'd have to plow his little ass over too! Gotta Deebo sometimes.* (Deebo was the neighborhood bully in the movie, *Friday,* who just took what he wanted and never asked permission.) That brings some laughter from the others who know that Gabe is just joking around. Shelly is shoveling the stoop and is having some difficulty with a part that has iced over. Suddenly, he slips and falls. When he looks up, he looks directly at his brother but hesitates for a moment. Alby looks away and just ignores him. Cruz asks if he is alright and automatically Alby shakes his head, because as a response to the question, Shelly immediately begins to cry.

Alby-*Why did you have to ask him that?* He explains that if they just would have ignored him, he would have been fine. *Once you make a big deal about it, he's gonna cry…You're alright, Shelly.* He tells his brother then looks at the others and rolls his eyes. Brixx approaches and brushes the snow off of Shelly's back and shoulders. He looks back at her and smiles while the tears continue to roll down his face. That is not the only thing that continues to fall. Shelly's nose is running and it is getting more noticeable and thicker. This forces Brixx out of her compassionate, nurturing mode and brings her back to the defensive teenager.

Brixx-*Wipe yur nose, geez!* It gets a laugh from the guys, but that was not what she was looking for. As soon as the words escape her mouth, she instantaneously regrets it.

Alaine- "Crazy love"

The group continues to work arduously and begins to discuss an event that transpired last week involving one of their neighbors. A twelve year old boy who is always in trouble had found it once again. He and some friends stole a car and were being chased by police. They evaded them for almost an hour, weaving in and out of the alleys in the projects before smashing the car into a parked van. They all ran away on foot and were later apprehended.

Gabe-*That boy is nuts! He's gonna be a serial killer, I'm telling you.* He states with his eyes open as wide as can be.

At that precise moment, a car speeds down the street and spins out about three times before coming to a halt. The passenger's side door abruptly opens and a man runs out, not bothering to shut the door. The man has a look of terror in his eyes, as the driver's side door opens and a woman leaps out in pursuit. The man has a good lead but the woman is much faster. They are screaming at each other at the top of their lungs. As they run, the man slips and loses some ground before she catches up to him and grabs hold of his wrists with both hands. He struggles to free himself, but her kung fu grip is overpowering; he cannot release her grasp on him as he exerts all his energy. Perhaps as a last resort, he head-butts her! The woman's head snaps back and she does not appear hurt, only stunned. The guys are now hysterical as the man rushes away like a hostage who has outsmarted his captors from a brainwashing cult. Once the woman regains her composure, she pursues her prey down the street screaming at the top of her lungs. The guys watch with their mouths wide open. She is quite fast and narrows the distance before they turn the corner and are out of sight.

Alby-*Looks like they're just as crazy here in the suburbs.* They continue to watch the couple as they get smaller and smaller. *They just left their car, too.* The car remains in the middle of the street with both doors wide open. *Man, did you see that head butt. That looked like professional wrestling!* Brixx was impressed with how fast the woman was and uses it to prove a point about women being just as good athletically as men.

The boy in the house watched the entire incident, yet he didn't find if amusing; the screaming and shouting simply reminded him of his own parents arguing and how in some twisted way he internalizes it and blames himself. If he was a better boy, perhaps they would not be fighting, he tells himself. Yet once again, this is never validated or denied. He looks at the laughing boys outside and wishes he could get the joke; he wishes he could be just part of the group, a part of anything, instead of being alone and lonely, like always.

Chris Rivers- "32 Shotz"

With his tongue hanging out of his mouth, Shelly almost finishes the stoop and is feeling rather proud of himself. He grabs a handful of snow and hits Alby with a snowball; this leads to an all out snowball fight. The envious boy watches with envy from his window, trying to remember the last time he played with anyone other than his nanny. Immediately, he goes to his closet and puts on his boots, knit hat, and winter coat; he is going outside to join the others he tells himself firmly. As the wind comes in from the east, Diego pulls his scarf over his neck and mouth. A warm feeling subconsciously engulfs him as he smells the laundry detergent that his Grandmother uses. It is a familiar smell that brings him comfort and puts a smile on his face. On some very deep level, that smell signifies to him that someone cares about him, even though he probably will never acknowledge or be aware of that. Inside, the boy's boots are untied and his jacket unbuttoned; neither has ever seen the world outside. As he makes his way downstairs, however, he forgets something and has to stop and pause. In his haste, he has forgotten gloves, so he runs back upstairs to his room to gather them. He is adamant that he is going to play with those boys; he has made his mind up.

Shelly-*I'm hungry, Alby. What are we gonna have for supper?* Alby rolls his eyes as he shakes his head, thinking out loud. *Shit, we just ate.* Drew pegs Diego in the back of the head with a small piece of ice. Gabe points at Shelly with two fingers, extending them fully, then gives him a solemn stare.

Gabe-*Man, you better just keep working and be quiet or I know what you're gonna have for dinner.* He continues to look at Shelly but now lowers his fingers.

Shelly-*What?* He waits eagerly for an answer to what he will have for dinner tonight.

Gabe-*Sleep!* Gabe stares him down and says not another word. Shelly's eyes begin to water up and Alby must come to his rescue. Meanwhile, Brixx attempts to come to Shelly's rescue trying to shove snow in Gabe's face, but he thwarts the attempt like a royal food taster in medieval times.

Alby-*He's just kidding, I dunno what's for dinner but after a couple more houses we'll go get a snack or something, Okay, but only if you stop complaining and work.* Without any more prompting, Shelly resumes working, avoiding Gabe's vicious stare, already thinking what he might get as a snack. He decides what he would like, but rather than interject once again, he just keeps his thoughts to himself for the moment. Cruz hits Alby on his neck with a handful of packed snow, and the snow falls down the back of his jacket, under his shirt. This simple act makes his little brother cheer up and laugh.

Just as they are finishing up, a Cadillac Escalade pulls into the driveway. The front door opens and an elegant woman exits, arms full of bags from Sax Fifth Avenue. The guys look in awe as she walks inside without so much as acknowledging their presence.

Diego-*That's what I'm talking about.* He begins staring at the SUV with his mouth wide open. Cruz and Drew walk up to the car and peer inside like two Peeping Toms. Drew is breathing so hard, he is fogging up the window and draws a piece sign in it. They discuss the features that the car must have. Gabe and Diego discuss how much that car costs while the others join in the discussion. Inside, the nanny catches the boy running to the front door in mid stride like a shortstop fielding a ground ball.

Nanny-*Oh no, where do you think you're going?* He looks at her in wonder. *No way are you going outside. Those boys have work to do; they're not here to play with you.* He seems offended by the remarks. His head drops and his body language changes completely. *You still have some reading to do anyway in that grammar book.* She sends him back upstairs and he walks with his head down. As he creeps up one step at a time, he hears his mother enter the house and he immediately stops at the halfway point of the staircase.

While the mother makes her way into the kitchen with her shopping bags, her son comes flying downstairs to greet her. Before he gets to the end of the staircase, he jumps on the polished banister and slides down on his stomach. He runs up and hugs his mother around her waist and she responds not with joy but rather annoyance.

Mom-*Careful, hon, I just got my nails done…*She makes sure not to give him a warm embrace in return. Instead of looking in her sons eyes, she stares directly at her newly primed nails which are sparkling and gleaming; she looks so pleased and forgets her son is even directly in front of her. Her hands go above his head to prevent him from touching her nails.

Son-*Mom, do you want to play cards?* The look on his face is filled with yearning; if she would only take a moment to notice.

Mom-*Maybe later, I'm exhausted. The lines in Sax were full of savages…I hate when they allow such rubbish in there…*As she continues talking, she takes her packages upstairs, ignoring her impressionable son. The nanny, upon seeing her lack of parenting skills, tells the boy to sit down while she makes him a roast beef sandwich. The look on his face tells it all, as he slouches in the chair. He remembers a time when he used to have temper tantrums for no apparent reason and his parents had to restrain him from hurting himself or damaging any of the household items. The doctors labeled him with Intermittent Explosive Disorder as well as Attention Deficit Hyperactivity Disorder. As a result, he was prescribed medications. What nobody failed to recognize, however, was that his tantrums were neither the result of explosive rage nor his uncontrollable urges to respond to multiple stimuli. It was the result of his craving for love and affection; when he would go into his fit, subsequently he would be restrained. Even though it was not a strong embrace or a symbol of love, it was nonetheless, physical contact which was something he desperately desired and required. Although he has changed his unhealthy behavior patterns, his mother and father have continued theirs. The nanny asks him if he wants swiss or american cheese on the roast beef. He just shrugs his shoulders in indifference.

Remy Martin- "Tight"

The group finishes up very efficiently, gets paid, and searches out some more work. The boy in the house watches as his brand new friends disappear behind the parked cars on the corner. He hopes they will return tomorrow. He has his winter outfit hidden on the side of his bed if they do. This time, he tells himself, he is going to sneak out the back door and go play with his new friends. He inspects his attire and makes sure he has his boots, gloves, scarf, and hat all prepared.

The group has been conscientiously working, and in the process, working off a lot of calories; hunger has once again set in. After three more houses, they decide to go get something to snack on since they are all almost on empty by now. They find a corner deli and enter. Inside, it is warm and the smells are a plethora of stews and soups. Drew goes to the counter first and orders some chicken noodle soup with crackers. Diego gets a healthy snack: some nacho cheese Doritos and a Mountain Dew. Brixx orders a bowl of chili with a green tea. She flashes back some years ago. Her father, who referred to himself as a weekend chef, would often make chili in the winter. He would chop up the onions and peppers so fine, they couldn't be detected by the human eye. He would always make it tasty, but not spicy. She would always add some hot sauce to make it hotter, which would always make her father laugh. After the man collects her money, she walks toward the door with her hot bowl in hand. After she dips her spoon into the bowl, she tastes the chili and walks back to the counter to ask for some hot sauce to put in it. Diego and Cruz notice this, and nod their heads in agreement at her walk on the spicy side. After she drops the hot sauce in the chili, she tastes it and with a smug look on her face says to herself, *Just like Dad's, always scared to put a lil heat in it.* Alby and Shelly are next in line and before the man behind the counter can ask, Shelly interjects.

Shelly-*I want some shells…and a scooter pie!* He states firmly and loud. The man behind the counter looks confused until Alby explains it to him. Around the way, at the deli where they are regulars, shells are simply pasta shells with tomato sauce, and Alby orders a half a pound so they can share. Scooter pies are a version of moon pies named after NY Yankees shortstop Phil "Scooter" Rizzuto; they have two graham crackers sandwiching marshmallow and covered in chocolate. The man behind the counter points to where the scooter pies are located and gives Shelly a wink.

<u>Man behind the counter</u>-*What else?* Cruz gets a hot chocolate and the biggest bag of Cheetos. *What else?* Seeing this Gabe makes a joke.

<u>Gabe</u>-*Now we know why your ding-a-ling is orange, son!* It takes the others a minute to get it, before they bust out laughing. Even the man behind the counter gets a kick out of that one and chuckles aloud.

<u>Cruz</u>-*No, now you know why your sister's ass is orange!* They laugh as Gabe acknowledges the beat down. The man behind the counter looks Gabe in the eyes and asks him the same question; they are exactly the same height.

<u>Man behind the counter</u>-*What else?* Gabe orders a turkey and cheddar sandwich on a Kaiser roll with extra mayonnaise. To wash it down he orders an extra large hot chocolate.

<u>Alby</u>-*Some snack, you act like you really worked hard or something.* Alby wonders if Gabe is going to retaliate, but realizes he is out of ammunition and just laughs. Shelly is in the corner of the deli devouring the shells like a starving man with his last meal. Alby reminds him unequivocally that if he spoils his appetite for dinner, he better not blame it on Alby. In his mind, he weighed the whining of his brother versus the scolding of his mother. Even though his mother's wrath is much harsher, he decided to go with the former, since he didn't want to hear neither his brother's rants nor his friend's smart-ass remarks. Even though he knows he's going to hear it later, he gives in to Shelly's hunger and decides he will deal with his mother later. After all, it is easier to ask for forgiveness rather than permission.

Ghostface Killah-"All that I need is you"

Once they all get their supplies, rather than head outside into the stark reality of winter, they huddle in the corner with Shelly and feast on their well earned fortifications. Brixx has finished her chili and again has pulled out that picture she drew in science class. She scrunches up her nose before she shoves it carelessly back in her back pocket. She throws her trash in the garbage and grabs Shelly's wrapper he left on the table to throw that out as well. Before the last morsel of artificial nutrients is consumed, Diego suggests they get back to the grind; they all agree, zip up their coats, wrap the scarfs around their necks, refit their winter hats and gloves, and make their way out of the sanctuary of home-made and processed goodies. As soon as the door opens, the wind sneaks up on the guys and smacks them dead in the face like a jealous lover. With them squinting their eyes, they brave the elements and walk single file, shovels over their shoulders like soldiers going back into battle against an unknown enemy.

Simultaneously, they all begin to think about home, the smells, the sounds, and all the familiar nuances that indicate to them that it is home. Diego smells his grandmother's home-made soup she makes with fish heads and an array of spices. Alby thinks of how warm he feels when he is in his bed, under his three blankets, after his mother comes in to make sure he has brushed his teeth, before she tells him to sleep tight and don't let the bedbugs bite.

Gabe thinks how good that couch he sleeps on would feel right at this moment, even with a spring or two jabbing him in his side. Drew thinks about the puzzle that he and his parents have started a couple of days ago which is supposed to be an Amazon jungle scene with wild animals; they are half-way finished and with supposedly 10,000 pieces, it will take them at least two more days to complete. Drew's parents always have family activities like this planned, even though Drew would never admit to liking such things as puzzles around his boys. Drew is a whiz at putting things together, whether it is a puzzle, television stand, or a carburetor. It is a natural talent that his parents encourage and nourish.

Cruz thinks about how many phone calls he has missed already from his sister; he doesn't want her to worry about him even though she knows his itinerary for the day. He can hardly wait to see her face when he shows her all the money he has earned today from a hard day's work. He knows how tired she is after working long hours at the hospital, and figures he should buy her something before he returns home to make her day just a little bit brighter. He knows how much she sacrifices to take care of him, and even though it is not her responsibility, she has taken it upon herself to do the job their parents were unwilling to do.

Brixx thinks about showing her mother all the money she has earned today. However, the realization that her mother probably couldn't tell a one dollar bill from a five at the moment causes her to pause. Her mother's eyesight is diminishing considerably and rather quickly at that. She looks forward to reading to her mother tonight. They are in the middle of a Toni Morrison book about some character from Harlem in the 1920's. Her mother loves anything from this particular author. Before she reads to her, she will comb her hair. When she was a child, her mother would comb and braid her hair. Nowadays, she combs her mother's hair which has turned almost half grey. This act of kindness makes Brixx feel wanted and needed. The others get that warm feeling from something their caretakers do for them. Brixx, however, gets that same feeling not from getting, but from giving. This is something vital that will separate her from the majority in her adulthood. Actually, it will be something that will single her out as rather unique.

Reef the Lost Cauze- "Eyes of My Father"

Crossing the busy street, they pass an alley and as they peer down the narrow passageway, they see a man and a woman smoking a pipe and passing it to and fro between them.

Diego-*Fuckin' crackheads, they're everywhere.* He states it with certitude as they all shake their heads in agreement. This is an all too common sight in the real world they live in. Gabe stares a bit longer than the rest, thinking about his mother. After all, that could be her for all he knows, just another victim falling prey to the all mighty rock. He knows that everyone succumbs for a multitude of reasons, and figures they are all feeble and puny.

Gabe-*Weak muthafuckas.* He whispers beneath his breath. In his mind, he considers the strains his mother must have been under and the choices she had to make. Also in the crevices of his subconscious lurk questions that are now slithering to the conscious like a serpent through a sewer. *Why mom? Why were you so weak? Why couldn't you be strong? Why couldn't you push it away? Why couldn't you get help? Why did you choose the pipe over your own son? What did I do wrong? If you just told me, I wouldn't have done it anymore. Was I that bad? Was it that hard? Do you still love me? Do you? Do you...*The inquisition continues without any clarification. It rolls over in his head like a gerbil on a wheel in its cage; that is how he often feels, like a caged rodent spinning aimlessly, round and round, going nowhere, searching for an exit. Out of breath and exhausted, without a way to escape, he ends up at the exact same spot he started in; after miles upon miles of running, searching, and longing, he is listless, sluggish, and stagnant.

A truck speeds by splashing slush all over the boys. They respond by shouting and cursing at the driver who raced away without any inkling of what he did.

Cruz-*Asshole!* He gives the driver the finger and wipes some slush off of his pants and jacket. Gabe snaps out of his instant funk and looks himself over. He giggles as he sees he is slush-free, the only one of the group to have come away unscathed.

Gabe-*Sometimes you're the dog, other times you're the hydrant.* He laughs at the others, pointing and relishing at his good fortune.

Turning right at the corner, they immediately begin looking for more prospective clients. They stumble upon a home with a chandelier over their front door. The porch raps around the home and seems to disappear into the darkness. There are twelve steps leading to the front door and a ramp winding back and forth three times before it meets the porch. Drew's blinking has become perpetual as he keeps his hands in his pockets. Brixx and Gabe are dumbfounded as they look on in bewilderment. *I thought people only had chandeliers inside the house, I never seen one on the outside… dam, they must be rich.* Cruz hits Drew on his chest with his glove which causes Drew's blinking to suddenly cease for the moment; they organically give each other a dap and push their way to the front of the group. Shelly immediately tells Alby that he is sizzling hot; Alby rolls his eyes and wipes Shelly's forehead with his glove which is soaking wet and cold. Temporary relief is brought to his little brother and silence prevails for one of the few times this afternoon.

Bebo Valdez and Diego el Cigala-
"Lagrimas Negras"

In the blink of an eye
It all changed
On the job for 17 years
Knock on wood
I lasted that long
Until that early winter morning
I could see it happening in slow motion
While everyone else was oblivious
Stirring their starbucks
Checking their Facebook on their iPhones
And definitely not making any eye contact
I could see the plot unfolding
And how that leads me here I still can't comprehend
Not only did I witness a tragedy
I was a participant
A perpetrator
How can one be all those things simultaneously?
Riddled with guilt
I have never been the same
Normally, point A to point B is a straight line
However, this zigzag journey befuddles me to no end

That poor woman
She looked right at me
Right through me
With such terror
We made eye contact
And I was helpless, frozen
Like a squirrel in the middle of the street
But I wasn't the one about to be crushed
There was nothing I could do but apply the brakes

She was pushed and I could do nothing
But I was the one who ultimately killed her
She became pinned underneath my train
Because I could not stop in time
I replay that in my mind every night
EVERY NIGHT!
And it always ends the same exact way
I know I am not to blame
Yet I am literally overflowing with guilt
Like lava abounding from a volcano uncontrollably

How that led to this
Only Freud knows
Because I sure don't
They say there is nothing physically wrong with me
That I should be able to get up and walk
But I am unable
I am helpless
I am stuck
Been sentenced to this chair
As my penance perhaps
For a crime I didn't commit
If I could walk again
It wouldn't be a miracle
Because I don't know if I would live my life any differently
I couldn't return to work
I just can't do it any longer
The gloom of the subway tunnels
The sudden flash of artificial lights
As I come around a bend towards the platform
The mass of people inching closer
Towards the edge as I approach
The unexpected
A disturbed individual
A person pinned in a corner and at their wit's end
A man who sees no hope
A woman who sees no reason to go on
Anyone fed up with the system
Can push an unaware victim to their certain death

Or jump on the tracks to touch the third rail
Like a small child at a petting zoo
Or wait anxiously for an end to their discomfort
Which ironically will be preceded by excruciating
Unimaginable pain
What must go through their minds
For those last fleeting moments
Do they think of their families?
Their regrets, their choices?
I can't even imagine
And I truly don't want to even try
I am already filled with so many things
Just like a piñata
Until you beat it out of me
Anything can fall out
Anxiety, guilt, fear, angst, worry, apathy, terror
Or some combination of any or all
So now I hang just like that piñata
Still, unable to move
With a continuous loop projecting in my head
Over and over
And over

REKS- "25TH Hour"

Shelly finally has the look of vindication on his face. He asks aloud why there is a ramp leading to the stoop and wishes he had one back home; his building is not wheelchair accessible and therefore, not up to code. Drew looks at Alby and recognizes he is blinking quite a bit from the expression on Alby's face. He takes a moment and concentrates to force himself to stop. Brixx and Gabe now take front and center as they prepare their spiel which has gotten very good over the course of the day. Brixx noticed the name, Eastman, over the mailbox which is number 129, and decides to give this a personal touch. Gabe rings the doorbell and looks around at his group to make sure they are well groomed and smiling; they are kings of marketing after only one day.

The door opens and the group is startled to see a woman in a wheelchair. Uncomfortably, they stare for a brief moment before Brixx asks the lady if she would like her driveway shoveled.

<u>Brixx</u>-*Mrs. Eastman, would you like us to shovel your driveway for you?* She opens up her eyes wide, looking innocent and irresistible. Diego and Drew wonder how she knew the lady's name. Regardless, they are very impressed and think they should do research before every house to give it that intimate touch. Cruz looks at the wheelchair and some vocabulary words come to mind. He knows his sister is going to quiz him this evening in some manner, so he wants to impress her and really wow her. *Incapacitate* is one of the words he hears the woman say and repeats it under his breath slowly, pronouncing each syllable with such precision meticulously... *incapacitate...*She continues to talk and he hears more wondrous words like *invalid, archaic*, and *deficient*. Cruz slowly pronounces each word in his head. *Archaic* slips out his mouth; Gabe catches wind of it and wonders what he is doing. He focuses his attention back to the prospective client giving her his undivided attention.

<u>Mrs. Eastman</u>-*Well, my husband will be home from work and it would save him the trouble...*She thinks about it with the door wide open and the boys can see right into the hallway and living room. In the hall, there are statues that look like they belong in a museum. Sculptures without arms, and paintings with old people scare Diego. He remembers seeing pictures of them inside some book in school and they always disturbed him. The living room has hand carved tables and chairs with yet another chandelier hanging above a long, glass table. Each chair must have been

measured to be equidistant from one another. The backs of the chairs are high and covered with satin. While Mrs. Eastman and Brixx come together on a price, Diego stares in both amazement and fear, into the home. A picture of an old man with a pipe in his mouth has made eye contact with him and he just can't shake it. Unbeknownst to the rest of the crew, he takes a few steps backwards down the stoop. Nobody notices.

Mrs. Eastman inherited the home with all the furniture and art inside from her grandmother. She is not wealthy by any stretch of the imagination, yet her home is impressive even to the amateur eye. Mrs. Eastman has a deep voice and when strangers call her, they always assume she is a man. Across the room from the painting that is haunting Diego at the moment is another painting of a woman standing on the ground and being pulled in opposite directions from above and below by two human-like figures. Above them is a hand acting as a tree with flowers. As one pans down, the arm turns into a river with rocks on both sides. There is a figure on the ground pulling a red wagon walking towards a piano. There are two spirits watching as the giant hand holds a needle and appears to be sewing up a heart with a castle within. Mrs. Eastman glances at the painting and now sees how that painting relates to her current situation. She is being pulled in many different directions and does not feel like she has any control over her life currently; she interprets it very differently right now. Diego takes some deep breaths and forces himself to focus and understand there is nothing to fear at the moment. Of course, the matter of the school bully, Davis, wanting to kick his ass may be upon him as early as tomorrow. He sees the other painting with three people pulling on each other over a huge red heart and it causes him to open his mouth. He looks around and is surprised nobody made a joke at how long his mouth was indeed open. He giggles to himself.

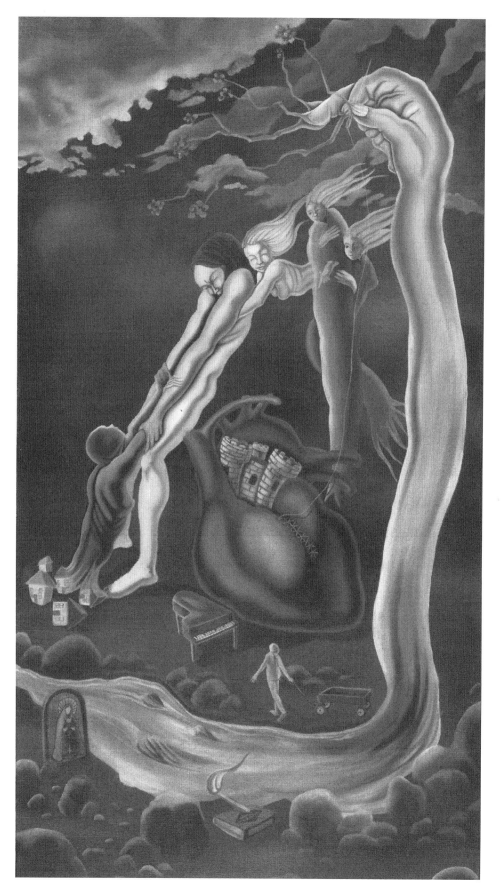

This painting was done in response to a recurring dream Mrs. Eastman had as a child; the dream and recurrent painting bring a tremendous amount of tranquility to her. Even though she has not had that dream in quite some time, it sooths her each and every time she passes by it. She wishes she would have that dream now as an adult. Oh, what she wouldn't give to have that dream tonight and every night, instead of the nightmares she has been possessed by. Her nights are no longer carefree slumber; those days are long gone. Now they are consumed by sleepless nights. She worked for the N.Y. Transit Authority for 17 years as a train operator. One horrendous day, someone was pushed on the tracks in front of her train, and she could not stop in time; the person was trapped under the train and died later that day. Two days after the incident, Mrs. Eastman lost all feeling below the waist and was from that day forward bound to that wheelchair.

Statistics report that three people die every month in that same manner in the N.Y.C. subway system. Coincidentally or not, the transit code for a passenger under a train is called a 12-9. Mrs. Eastman's address is 129. She never put it together before, but now believes it was indeed foreshadowing. If that passenger is killed, the operator gets three days off from work. If the passenger is not killed, it is dealt with on a case by case basis. In addition to the operator having a massive amount of guilt, he or she must take a urine test to see if there are any drugs or alcohol in his or her system within two hours of the incident.

Tito Puente- "El Cumbanchero"

Diego and Drew stare at the woman who is looking beyond the group by now. They wait for an answer as the woman just stopped in mid-sentence while talking to Brixx about the price. Brixx is patient and after looking to Gabe pushes her hand to the ground indicating they should just wait for the woman to come back from wherever she has gone. Diego takes a step back and closer to his bodyguard, Gabe, unbeknownst to the both of them. The look in Diego's eyes goes unnoticed by everyone but Mrs. Eastman. She recognizes that look as terror, and is brought back in time. That woman had a similar look times about 1,000! She just can't shake it. No matter how many nights go by, no matter how many methods she tries, no matter how many people tell her otherwise, she still feels responsible.

She stares at the painting and interprets everything in it to that woman. Perhaps that woman had a small child who played with a red wagon. Perhaps that woman was an up and coming musician in a fancy piano bar. Perhaps she was devoutly religious and on her way to church to sing in the choir. Oh, if only someone was watching over, ensuring she could be safe on that particular day. If only someone was there to rescue her and pull her to safety. If only someone prevented the entire atrocity by snatching that woman before she fell to her untimely and ultimately last moment on this earth. If only… Her mind races like two children on the playground during recess. She is in another place entirely and has totally forgotten about the children at her doorstep. Diego, still drawn to the painting, simply can't look away. Now he sees that Mrs. Eastman is looking directly into his eyes and that makes him feel even less comfortable. He forces himself to think of something pleasant and moves further down the stoop so he is the closest to the street just in case he needs to run away. Nobody else seems to be bothered by the painting and Diego momentarily thinks he has lost his mind. He thinks of his grandfather who always calls him, *El cubanchero*. It is a slang word his grandfather constantly uses which means a person who likes to have fun and knows how to have a good time. He chuckles to himself and realizes he is being silly. That painting is not going to come alive. He takes a step closer to the house and now is on equal ground with Shelly. He chuckles again aloud and thinks that if the man from the painting does, by some miraculous fashion come alive, and start chasing him, he would run away and let Shelly be the sacrificial lamb. He knows he can outrun Shelly and the man will just catch him and do his will. By that time, he will be long gone. He chuckles once again but louder which causes Shelly to look his way and begin chuckling with him. Together they share a first-rate giggle, however, only one of them knows what they are snickering about. Finally, Mrs. Eastman snaps out of it and they agree on a price and the group begins working. Diego, however, is still haunted by that painting. He keeps looking over his shoulder to make sure the man in that picture isn't coming alive and after him. He watched some movie on TV recently with his grandfather where a painting came to life, then stalked and killed a couple that moved into the home.

Cruz-*What's wrong with you?* He notices Diego acting peculiar and wants to help. Gazing off into the distance, Diego shrugs it off and resumes working. Diego's grandmother argued with his grandfather and was adamant about him not watching that movie. It will give him nightmares, she had said. At the time, he thought it was nonsense. Now he is beginning to think perhaps she was right.

Drew suggests when they get all their money for the day they wait for a nice day and have a big barbecue and invite all their friends and families.

Alby-*Man, I don't wanna hang out with all those fools!* Drew asks why. *Cause you know if we have a big barbecue people gonna come eat all our food.* Drew explains that's the plan. Gabe reminds them of the block party they had last summer when Davis and his family crashed their barbecue. *Yea, that's right, and they don't even live in our projects.* Cruz and Drew ask them to jog their memory. Alby and Gabe begin to laugh. *They came over with like eight people and then made a plate to go. They were looking around for tin foil, and there was no more left, so they went to that white van of theirs.* Diego remarks that their van looks just like a child molester van your mother warns you about when you are little. *When they came back, that old snaggletooth family had a whole roll of tin foil. Davis so greedy they planned to take some of **our** food home with them.* They all remember now and begin to laugh, even Diego. Between the man in the painting and the threats from Davis in school, Diego needs a good laugh. *Eating all them ribs and chicken and I damn sure don't know how that fool, Davis, ate that corn on the cob with only four good teeth.* He demonstrates how that is possible and eats an imaginary ear of corn pretending he is missing teeth. *He must use that snaggletooth as a can opener for the beans!* Everyone is laughing so loud at that and Diego is the loudest of the bunch. Mrs. Eastman rolls herself to the window and peaks out in response to the entire ruckus. She is so envious of the group and wishes she could relax and unwind for just a moment. Brixx is the only one who notices they are being watched, so she barks for everyone to get back to work. Alby doesn't appreciate being ordered around and tells the group what's on his mind.

138

<u>Alby</u>-*Man is she getting bossier every minute or is it just me?* Diego and Gabe start to laugh at Alby while Shelly disagrees with his big brother.

<u>Shelly</u>-*It's just you. I think she is nice.* He smiles at the group and isn't ashamed he went against his brother who can only shake his head.

Chucho Valdes and Concha Buika- "Soledad"

As everyone works vigorously, Gabe is lecturing the group on making sure the minute details of their work are completed correctly.

<u>Cruz</u>-He has been waiting for the perfect time to use his word of the day. Before he left the house, he pulled his word calendar up and tore off today's word, *pedantic*. He studied the definition at least three times and knows exactly what it means. The dictionary stated: *overly concerned with minute details, especially in teaching.* He waits for a moment then tells Gabe what he thinks. *We understand what we gotta do, stop being pedantic about it!* He looks to the ground and shovels a large sheet of ice, throwing it over his shoulder. The others, fully aware of what he is doing just stop in unison and stare at him. Cruz pretends he doesn't notice and continues to heave snow and ice over his shoulder. Eventually, after continued silence, he stops and straightens up with a smile on his face. *What?* He looks around for a response. *Would you prefer I use the word, didactic? Okay, Gabe stop being so didactic, wouldya. We got work to do.* Again, he resumes working as the others just bust out laughing. Cruz knows they don't know the words, shoot, neither did he before today. Didactic is a synonym of pedantic and he memorized that this morning as well; it was on the reverse side of the paper with pedantic. Its definition is *inclined to teach or lecture others too much.* Cruz seems very proud of himself as the others in unison bonk him with snowballs. He picks up some snow and hits Diego and Drew respectively. He looks at Brixx and packs a snowball and winds back. She points a finger at him and has a word for him today herself.

<u>Brixx</u>-*You hit me with that snowball, you walking dictionary, and I'll kick your sorry derriere down this street and back to the ghetto!!* He stares for a moment and tosses the snowball aside. *Or would you rather me say posterior? That's right; you ain't the only one in school fool.* The laughs grow louder and louder. Alby watches from a distance not wanting any piece of Brixx; he can see she is a worthy adversary.

Bobby Darin- "Beyond the Sea"

Inside the house, Mrs. Eastman is lonely and comes out on the porch which is free from snow. Brixx sees her come out and wonders if anything is wrong. She approaches the lady and asks if she needs something.

<u>Mrs. Eastman</u>-*No, honey, just wanted a bit of fresh air.* She takes in a deep breath and watches the smoke from her exhalation escape from her lips as she sighs. *Where are you from?* Brixx tells her that they are from the Bronx, but she is originally from Queens. *Ah, you certainly appear to be a little queen, dear.* That makes Brixx smile and turn away blushing. They begin discussing food and in particular, bagels, pizza and Chinese food.

One thing New Yorkers can always talk about and agree to disagree upon is food, especially those things which differentiate New York from the rest of the world. Three things that New York makes the best are bagels, pizza, and Chinese food. When New Yorkers move out of New York, those are definitely the three things they miss the most. If two strangers meet in any other city other than New York, and realize that they are both from that city so nice they named it twice, inadvertently, those three items will bond them like no other. That's a guarantee! Different theories abound: some say it is the water because it is so hard, some say it is an art form that only exists there, and some theorize it is the multitude of ethnicities that all coexist. Whatever it is, it is something distinct that connects one city like no other.

Mrs. Eastman and Brixx are now bonding over the aforementioned topic. Brixx tells her where they ate for lunch and that it was delicious. She tells her about a place around the corner named *Zsa Zsa's* which is superb. Brixx tells her about this Chinese restaurant that her father used to take her to back in Queens that had these tiny Mandarin spare ribs that were to die for. Mrs. Eastman asks Brixx about her upbringing and she is surprisingly forthcoming. Brixx in turn reluctantly, yet innocently, asks her customer why she is in a wheelchair. Gabe and Diego witness Brixx chatting up the customer and comment how that is great for business. Alby turns his nose up at Brixx's rise in popularity among the group, even though it is hard to deny. Mrs. Eastman, who has always been hesitant for anyone to broach that subject, tells her the entire story. She spills her guts to Brixx, telling her about the accident, and her feelings surrounding the events that followed. This, in and of itself, is so cathartic for Mrs. Eastman, that afterwards, she feels so unburdened, purified, and exhausted all at the same time.

After some superb active listening, Brixx quickly jumps back to it. Working at a painstaking pace, Diego looks to his left and to his right, ensuring he is safe from attackers. Alby looks around and sees Brixx doing just as much labor as the guys. Hmm, maybe she could be part of their faction. She stands straight up and stretches her back and spots him looking; he quickly looks away not wanting to make his acceptance evident. Drew is very happy to be around his friends. He is happiest when he is surrounded by love and that is what he feels at the moment. A smile gradually radiates over his face as he breathes in the winter air. Shelly glances around and burps loud enough for the group to hear. Everyone laughs which makes him feel happy. He looks to his brother who winks at him as he gets back to his work.

Billy Joel- "Pressure"

I'll never do it again
I swear it!

You know how many times I have said that?
I can't remember, that's how many
Yea, I lie
But that's not all
I also cheat and steal
Not only from strangers
From my friends and my family too
From everybody

So what
I have to
I have to get high
I have to get away
I have to get my fix
I have to

I never hurt anybody
Just myself
And I am accustomed to pain
Well, sometimes others do get hurt
But it's not my intention
It is, however, a byproduct
If they would just give me what I need
I'll be gone
In a flash
Just let me get high

143

It's a win-win proposition
For everyone else
Either I get high
And I am temporarily happy
And nobody is bothered
Or I will die and then they will be satisfied
I'll finally be out of their hair

Nobody is going to cry at my funeral
I know that
All I have caused is pain and misery
To me and anyone cursed enough to have cared
Nobody is going to miss me
Why would they
It should come as a welcomed relief
One less thing to worry about
One less stressful trigger
One less nightmare
They'll probably share a collective sigh of relief
And a glass of champagne
And I don't blame them
They will be better off
Because I am a mess
A complete and utter waste of space
And I know it

My mother should have aborted me immediately
Because I didn't ask to be brought into this miserable world
Full of hate, ignorance, greed, intolerance, and betrayal
But once I was engulfed with such poisons
I had no other choice but to breathe in the toxins
And become another parasite
That infests and kills everything in its path
Like a hurricane on the loose
Destroying everything in its path
That has taken years to build and develop

That's how I see myself
Out of control with no end in sight
And even when it seems I have turned a corner
And appear ready to make it all right
I just fuck it up yet again
That was just the eye of the hurricane
And before long
I am back to my basic nature
Of destruction, despair, and devastation
To anyone unfortunate enough to have been sucked into my path
To everyone who has ever reached out to me and attempted to make a difference
To each one who has ever fell victim to my charm
And actually believed the empty words that escaped
my procrastinating and diseased lips
And mostly to the disgusting figure I see before me in the mirror
Myself

I have crossed too many people
Correction, everyone
I have burned too many bridges
Correction, every bridge
I have let too many dreams go by unrealized
Correction, every dream
To think I can come back from this
At this point
Would be just one more lie to throw on the massive
heap of lies that have accumulated
Like piles of trash during a garbage strike
I have no more friends
No more family
And no more opportunities staring me down
I don't blame them
Not in the least
But I'm gonna get mine
I gotta do what I gotta do
Because this world is too painful
Too difficult
And too scary for me to face sober

For that reason and that reason alone
I run away
From anything that has ever been positive for me
And I run toward that which has destroyed my entire existence
But now, I see it not as my downfall
But the very foundation of my existence
It is the reason I get up in the morning
And the reason I even bother to inhale and take a polluted breath
Because without it
I can't breathe
I can't live
And I can't exist
So pardon my insolence
And my crassness
But either help me get high
Or get the hell out of my way

Sunz of Man- "Soldiers of Darkness"

Finishing with the Eastman house, the crew is rejuvenated and getting their second or third wind. Shelly leads the charge, burping again, and continuously looks back to ensure is brother is close by like a week old puppy with his new owner. He wipes his nose with his sleeve and points ahead to the next customer. At the end of the street, is a two story house with a big Ford F150 in the driveway and a boat in the backyard which is visible from the sidewalk; it is only half-way covered with a tarp. The name on the mailbox reads, *The Williams-Lane Family*, however the man residing inside is not the owner, not that Mr. Williams-Lane; he is his son. The mailbox is very inviting; it is an old trolley car made of wood and it has such tiny detail on it. Obviously, it was a custom-made mailbox. Alby grabs Shelly by the hood because he is lulling in the middle of the street and is almost hit by a passing motorist. Drew shakes his head and instructs his partners that this one is a gold mine. He explains that if the owner has a boat, he is probably loaded.

Inside, a man approximately 35 years of age has a pipe in one hand and a glass of stale gin in the other. As the smoke rises to the ceiling, he cocks his head back at the same time as his eyes glaze over. The thick white smoke dances like a ballerina under the light fixture attached to the ceiling. The glass in his hand begins to tilt and a few splashes of liquor fall onto the brand new hardwood floor below. He seems oblivious and doesn't even attempt to clean up the spill. Gabe taps his large knuckles against the oak door four times rapidly. There is absolutely no movement.

Cruz-*Knock again.*

Gabe-*Relax, tranquilo.* He throws a word in Spanish back to Cruz. *Nobody's home.*

Cruz-*But I hear music… knock louder.* Gabe presses his ear against the door and hears a steady beat penetrating from the back of the house. He takes a deep breath and knocks again, this time more thunderous and lengthier. The others laugh aloud at Gabe's obvious lack of patience. From inside, the man barely moves as he hears the knocking at the front door. It takes almost every ounce of strength he has in him to sit up straight. He takes a long swig from his glass. Even though there is no ice or juice, he doesn't even grimace before he finally stands up and massages his neck. The boys surrender, turn and walk down the stoop; they begin to look for another house, when the front door opens with ferocity. The man stares at the boys, yet fails to say a word. Gabe takes a step towards the man and asks if he wants his driveway shoveled. The man takes a long while to respond. Drew and Cruz look at each other and almost begin laughing. The boys think he is perhaps prejudiced or rude, when in actuality, he is trying to get his bearings and determine where he is. He remembers coming home last night about six after scoring some heroin uptown. After that, it's all a blur. Coming home is a bit of an understatement because this home doesn't belong to him. He grew up here and his parents now reside there without any of their children; they are down in Florida for a vacation and have no idea there home is being occupied. He rocks to and fro for a moment until his eyes dilate and he sees these teenagers in front of his house. Once he realizes what is going on, he likes the idea of someone doing the work that needs to be done by him; he always has. As he yawns with his mouth wide open, he doesn't bother to cover it. Seeing that his truck is completely boxed in by the snow, he sucks his teeth in disdain. He moves his tongue around in his mouth tasting last night's escapades before he asks them how much. Back and forth they discuss a price, and when it is finally agreed upon, the man unintentially slams the door shut. Again, the boys look at each other and laugh shrugging their shoulders. Returning to his chair, he lights up the pipe once again and falls back into his cocoon of obscurity.

The guys just stare at each other and laugh at the man's strange behavior. Diego and Gabe take a minute to compose themselves because they are laughing so hard. By now, the guys have their routine down to a science and within ten minutes, they have a third of the job completed. Diego unzips his jacket down to his waist, because he is beginning to perspire under his thermal shirt.

Diego-*You think they're gonna cancel school tomorrow?* He asks out loud to nobody in particular.

Alby-*I hope so, I got a test in social studies tomorrow and I couldn't give a shit about them fools in 1776!*

Cruz-*That's cause you're too busy playing poker in the back of the room.*

Drew-*Or shooting dice in the bathroom.* He smiles at Cruz.

Brixx-*Or looking at playboys and penthouse under the stairwell you horny pervert!* Diego laughs and points at Alby.

Alby-*Shit, I gotta get paid, don't I…and those magazines are art mind you.* He begins to laugh and suddenly the front door opens up as wide as it can. From the sidewalk, they can see all the way inside the man's house. Without closing the door, the man walks down the stoop and asks the boys to gather around. The heat from in the house escapes like bees from a disturbed beehive. From his pocket he takes out a gold chain.

Mr. Williams-<u>Lane</u>-*How about instead of the mula, I give you guys this sweet necklace…it's worth at least 50 bucks.* He looks the boys over and immediately Gabe declines the offer while Cruz seems to like the chain. Drew's blinking catches the man off guard for a moment, and then continues his pitch. Gabe, however, is not falling for the okey-doke.

<u>Gabe</u>-*Naw, we'll take the cash.* One more time, the man attempts to barter, unaware of Gabe's strong resolve.

Mr. Williams-<u>Lane</u>-*Well, how about for this ring.* He pulls a ring off his finger and it is gold and engraved.

<u>Cruz</u>-*What does it say on it?* He asks the man who changes the subject and offers the necklace and ring together as a package deal. The man begins to shiver because he is not wearing a coat, all he has on is a thermal shirt with a large orange stain on the front.

<u>Gabe</u>-*I think we'll just stick to the cash.* The man shakes his head in exasperation and walks back inside, slamming the door loudly behind him once again; this time the door slam was indeed intentional. *What is this, a fuckin' game show, give me busted up jewelry for $200 Alex.* Cruz tells the guys that the jewelry was probably worth more than the cash.

<u>Brixx</u>-*Yea, but maybe it's stolen or not his to give; we don't need any headaches today. Anyway, I don't trust the look in his eyes, something is goin on there.* The others agree in unison and now Gabe is overly concerned the man might not have the money to pay them when they are finished with the job. Drew wants to say something, but becomes aware of his blinking and focuses all his attention on stopping. He remembers what his mother had told him about being able to control it and he tries with all his might until he has it under control momentarily.

<u>Alby</u>-*Now, I'll take that boat for payment, I know that's worth a lot.* Shelly thinks he is serious and starts to jump up and down thinking they are going to have a boat. He wonders to himself how they are going to get that huge thing home, and where on earth they are going to put it.

Angel Canales - "Lejos de Ti"

Away from the group, Diego becomes very pensive; he noticed track marks on the man's neck, indicating that he has been doing drugs by shooting needles. The others did not notice, however, Diego has gotten to be somewhat of an expert at spotting drug users and the manner in which they attempt to conceal their little secrets. Unfortunately, the marks are just like the ones his mother and father had on their body. When he was younger, he would ask what the marks were and they would tell him an array of lies; all of them he believed willingly and without hesitation. Even when he knew the truth, he forced himself to believe the lies, unwilling and unable to believe his parents were both drug addicts. It got to be so bad that his father would shoot up between his toes and in his neck, while his mother would shoot up in any body part that remained unmarked.

Diego regresses to another time and place; he recalls how he would walk up his father's body until he would be able to do a flip like a gymnast. He would stand directly in front of his father, coming up to his stomach, and they would grab hold of each other's hands. Then slowly he would climb up his father's legs until he got to his stomach, then he would creep up further to his father's chest. Abruptly, he would push off with his feet and spin backwards, all the while holding on to his father's hands. At that point, he would spin back and laugh uncontrollably. There came a time where his father simply became too weak to hold Diego's weight any longer and that had to regrettably come to an end. Why did his father have to let go of his hand? *Why did he let go? Don't let go Dad! Don't let go of me! Don't let go!* Diego is lost in thought and precipitously bursts out startling his cohorts.

<u>Diego</u>-*Hey, you know that guy is shooting that shit!* They look on without words. *Heroin.* The others stare at him strangely. They ask if he is sure and he replies, *Yup!* They know the story of his parents and take his word for it, no need to question his experience on this issue. Nor do they bother to drum up the past by more questions on the subject matter. As quickly as it was brought up, the subject matter is dropped as they resume shoveling. Back inside, the man replenishes his drink as the phone rings. It takes him a couple of minutes to actually find the phone and when he does, he picks it up with jubilation.

<u>Man</u>-*Yea, yea, I know Jack…but. . . but…I told you I'd have it by Wednesday… no…tell you what, put me down for a grand on the number three horse in the third*

*at Yonkers…across the board, yea…I know, Jack…you know I'm good for it…yea…I will…I…*Apparently the person on the other end of the phone hung up because he looks at the phone for an instant before slamming it down. Guzzling his drink, he sits back down and looks around. Nothing seems recognizable while it all seems familiar at the same time. He is wearing a white and green baseball hat that has seen better days. The back is made of mesh, the lid has tears in it and has been bent and molded into a severe arch; it is not the style in New York, but more how the southerners wear their baseball hats. But then again, this gentleman has never fit in wherever he found himself. His skin is extremely pale; it looks likes there is no blood flow through his body because his skin has a bluish hue. He grabs a box of cereal from the pantry, opens it and pours it recklessly into an oversized bowl. Then he takes the box and slams it on top of the refrigerator not bothering to close the plastic wrapping or the box it originally came in. The milk he left out overnight has gotten warm and spoiled, yet that does not dissuade him in the least. He pours the sour milk over his meal and digs in with a tablespoon. The black and white checkered kitchen floor is now scattered with loose cereal and sour milk as he rubs his scruffy cheek; he has not shaved in five days and it is not even on his agenda for the next several days.

Mr. Williams-Lane was belittled, ignored, and put down as a child by his parents. They weren't awful parents, but they were simply not thoughtful or experienced parents. When he failed at something, which was natural, he was never encouraged and was made to feel like a failure and told he was just a loser. His low self-esteem got progressively worse, until as a teenager he began to use drugs and alcohol to ease the pain, which made him feel better about himself, even if it was momentarily. This led to a downward spiral that has continued until today. Every minute of every day is consumed by the use and abuse of drugs and alcohol. Believe it or not, for a while there, he was considering becoming a priest. That direction, however, was short lived. When he graduated high school, he was secretly voted most likely to climb a bell tower with a high-powered rifle and go postal!

Scarface- "Mary Jane"

As the entire group works relentlessly, they vocally hope this man has the money to compensate them for their hard work. From the sidewalk, the guys can hear the system inside cranking up to some classic rock music they don't recognize. The guitar solo wails through the cracks in the walls which parallel the wails coming from inside the young man. Talking out loud to himself, he begins to shout and throw things against the wall. Curse words are hurled alongside the glasses and plates that crash to the floor. Shelly is on the stoop and hears the ruckus, as he shouts to Alby, who rolls his eyes and instructs him to keep on working. Drew stops for an instant, leaving his shovel standing by itself sticking out of the ground. He wonders to the others if maybe they should just cut their losses and move on to the next house.

Gabe-*Hell no!* He figures they are almost finished and to stop now would be foolish. He begins to wonder to himself. *How can this guy have such a big house and a boat if he's on that shit?* The answers escape him; however, if the walls were made of any transparent or translucent material, he would be omniscient and be able to understand. Because inside, the man is thinking how his parents are going to react when they realize he has sold their car, their jewelry, and is attempting to sell the boat while they are away in Florida for the week. Then again, he doesn't contemplate it for long as he stumbles through the liquor cabinet looking for something else to quench his thirst. They have washed their hands of their son a long time ago, after being burned so many times. They have no idea he is in their house, and if they did, they would surely call the police, again. He was given numerous chances, and each and every time he screwed them over, not unlike everyone else in his life. No longer does he have a key to the home; the back bathroom window now is smashed in from a ceramic turtle his mother had in the garden. That is how he entered the house, so add breaking and entering to all his charges.

Tightening the belt around his bicep, he searches for the vein which by now has retreated like a turtle's head in its shell. With his vision blurry, he attempts to inject the bug juice and escape for an instant, a moment, an eternity, that will only last a second or two; however, those two seconds will be euphoria, transporting him to a place where nothing at all matters, a place where everything is everything. The only problem is when the transformation is complete, he turns back into that monster who is a sociopath, unrelenting, and poisonous. Mr. Williams-Lane flashes back to the only thing that brought him peace as a child: his fish. He was given a fish tank on his ninth birthday by his grandfather and he treasured those fish. Whenever he was hurt or angry, he would retreat to the comfort of his room and watch his fish. He would imagine he was in a carnival and had trained the fish to do tricks. They would do flips and swim in circles to please him. His grandfather was the only one who was ever patient with him. The only one who ever listened to him. He passed away four years after giving him the fish. Once his grandfather died, all he had was his fish. He would run home after school and close his bedroom door. There, he would spend hours upon hours of staring at his fish, thinking about his departed grandfather, and transforming himself to another place and time.

This type of parasite is not new to the boys; on the contrary, they are surrounded by them like wagon trains in an old black and white movie. But for some reason, they collectively believed that once you cross the imaginary line of the ghetto, and you make your way into the land that everyone strives to attain, the suburbs, with clean sidewalks, healthy trees, and wide streets, you magically travel to a land that is worry-free, trouble-free, and simply free. Moreover, almost everything they see on television, like Willy Wonka and the Chocolate Factory, is a fantasy. Nobody is immune to the parasites of today's world. The boys just took it for granted that it didn't rain on this side of the street. One day they will discover that both sides get equally wet, and puddles gather wherever it rains.

Paul McCartney and Wings- "Live and Let Die"

Suddenly the door swings open and the man rushes out with a racing form hanging out of the back of his stained blue jeans. With one hand in his pocket, he fumbles for his car keys and with the other he raises his plastic cup to his lips. Exhaling, the smoke from the bitter cold engulfs his face momentarily. As he reaches for an empty pack of cigarettes in his other pocket, he begins talking to himself aloud. Gabe is leaning against the house with one foot on the ground. When he sees the man exit the home, he pushes off with the foot resting against the aluminum siding and walks over to watch Brixx confront their customer. Drew and Diego see Gabe move without delay and they stop what they are doing to watch and listen.

Mr. Williams-Lane-*Hmm...maybe I better just go to OTB* (Off Track Betting)... He then directs his attention to the adolescents in the yard and looks at the boys... *Hey, you don't have a cigarette do you?* They all shrug no. *Say, do you think I can pay you guys tomorrow?* He attempts to work his charms on the boys, but unfortunately for him, they have seen it all before. His charms are like bootleg jewelry that has lost its shine. Brixx has been prepared for this and takes the initiative to speak for the entire group.

Brixx-*Listen, mister, we've been working out here in the cold for a half hour on your house and...*The man nods his head up and down and attempts once again to make a trade for some jewelry he pulls out of his coat pocket. Gabe walks over next to Brixx and makes sure the man does not try to dine and dash, like they have done countless times themselves. After a couple more failed attempts, he pays the boys in a wad of crumpled up one dollar bills and a handful of change that equals the bill. The man brushes up against Gabe by mistake and notices for the second time how intimidating this kid is. He excuses himself and walks away smiling a fake smile. Diego looks at Drew and Cruz as they all look to Gabe. He acknowledges their appreciation because they are pretty sure that if they were without him, they probably would not have gotten the man to pay up. The man backs the truck out of the driveway, and the boys can see the huge dent on the passenger's side door. Inside the truck, the man is fumbling around, looking in the glove compartment, the back seat, and in the cushions. Immediately, he runs over some bushes sticking out of the snow in the front yard and narrowly misses the mailbox. He waves at the boys who just nod at him as he peels away, skidding in the slushy street.

<u>Alby</u>-*Alright, no more crack heads, right?* They all begin to laugh as they make their way down the block, in search of another customer, a paying customer.

Shelly asks for the change because he likes the way the weight feels in his pocket, not to mention the jingling sounds. He has a huge smile on his face as the sweat falls from his forehead. Brixx turns to the guys and smiles and she all but knows she is now part of the group. The guys walk in unison down the street looking confident and laughing at their last customer.

The Beatles-"Eleanor Rigby"

I'm a prisoner
In my own home
In my mind
In my soul
A prisoner by my own devices
I can't leave ever
Even for a moment
If I do
I am overwhelmed by anxiety
Overrun by fear and detachment
Overwrought by the racing thoughts in my head
Overdrawn on my account of self-esteem

Sweat builds on my forehead
Like a pot of water
Just before it boils
My arms become glued to my sides
Like a dress shirt sticks to your back
When you get behind the wheel of your car
That has been sitting in the summer sun all day
My legs get heavier and heavier
Like a baby's eyes
When he is fighting sleep
My mouth gets so dry
Like a forest that has been without rain for months

Just to leave the house
You see what a chore it is
To you it is like taking a breath
For me it is like not being able to breathe

I am terrified to leave
And miserable to stay
Either way I am in a funk
That has lasted for many years
I feel like a deserted Ms. Havisham
But I am not waiting on my wedding day
I am not foolish enough to dream
I know that is not a possibility
Who would be foolish enough to imprison themselves?
With a fool who acts as his own guard and warden
Nobody and I know it

So that is how it has been and how it will be
For this shadow of a man
And I accept that
I am under no illusions
Under no misconceptions
I am, however, grateful for any company
No matter how bothersome
Jehovah witness, Girl Scout, or lost soul
Something to break the monotony
And give me just a simple touch
Of reality and the outside world
That I will never see again

Nettai Tropical Jazz Big Band- "Getaway"

Once the guys are halfway down the block, Diego glances back at the house, once again thinking about his own parents. He recalls how his father used to let him ride on his shoulders and Diego would cover his father's eyes and he would pretend to not be able to see and wander around aimlessly. Diego felt on top of the world being up so high, but apparently so did his father. With Diego on his shoulders, he would grab hold of his lovely wife, and the three of them would dance to the music on the radio, which was situated on top of the refrigerator. That same radio is the one his grandfather always listens to; he is unsure if it holds the same significant meaning to him as well.

Diego reflects back to his father's funeral, one month before his mother's. He was sitting with his grandparents and was in a complete daze. Although Diego didn't fully comprehend what had happened, he truly didn't want to realize the finality of the event. In his mind, his father would walk through the front door, carrying a toy truck or spaceship, and greet Diego like it was any other day. However, his father never did walk through that door again. Neither did his mother. After his father's funeral, his mother just disappeared and they received word from the police what had transpired. Since then, his grandparents have taken the place of his parents and have done one hell of a job. They understand how difficult it must be for Diego, even now, so they approach him with a lot of patience, but still with a load of discipline. Fate has snatched his parents from him like a chameleon snatches an insect on a tree limb. The last thing Diego's grandparents want is for their grandson to fall victim to the same destiny.

Quickly, the group completes two more houses without a hitch. Gabe has located the next house and begins to discuss the possible price with the fellas. Diego, however, is still adrift in his memory.

Gabe-*Yo, Diego, you with us?* He waits for a response and does not get one. He looks at Drew with a puzzled look on his face. *Shit, talk about ADD.*

Drew-*He ain't ADD, he's ABCDD!* The others laugh as Diego snaps back to the moment. Gabe walks up the steps and knocks on the door. The name by the mailbox says Mr. Hokato. When the door opens, they are surprised to see a huge man, who appears to be hiding behind the door, because he has only opened it up a few inches wide. They hear him talking to a dog and he doesn't want the dog to run outside. After a few words, they agree on a price and the boys immediately get to work. Inside, Mr. Hokato is excited to have someone who will shovel his driveway because today his sister and her children are coming to visit and he was wondering how they were going to pull into the driveway. One would think he could obviously do it himself, but he can not. Mr. Hokato has agoraphobia with panic disorder; this means he is struck by fear and anxiety whenever he leaves his home and goes anywhere in public. The anxiety usually shows itself in the form of a panic attack whereupon he cannot breath, his thoughts become all jumbled, and he simply panics. It is not a pretty sight and as a result, Mr. Hokato has not left his home in four long years.

For a while he did have a girlfriend; this was a surprise even for him, but it didn't last very long at all. Her name was Angel and she was a vegetarian. She had fits of anger and once spit in Mr. Hokato's face. His sister told him that he is better off without her. *That chick needs to eat a hamburger or a steak! All those veggies going to her head…She ain't right!* Mr. Hokato was his happiest when he was a child. He often wishes he could go back to those days and just wait for the ice cream man to buy a bomb pop. Those were his favorite; they were red, white and blue and took him almost an entire hour to eat. He would eat his bomb pop and dream of being a superhero with super powers. One day he would want to be invisible, the next day he would want the power to fly. He would swing on his swings and make himself go very high and then jump off at the top of his jump, pretending he was flying. His mother always wanted him to practice on the piano but he was not interested in that whatsoever. Almost every day, he wore these purple and blue velour sweat pants his grandmother made him; he wore them nearly every single day. His mother would get on him for constantly wearing them but he loved them, and loved the feel of velour against his skin. His grandmother promised to make him a velour cape to go with the pants. He wanted to fly, be invisible, and he wanted to be a superhero. Currently, he has made himself somewhat invisible because he is not seen by many people. However, presently he has no way near the capacity for flying.

He walks into the kitchen to make some hot chocolate and opens an Entenmann's Pecan Danish Ring to serve the kids to show his appreciation. Humming to himself, he pulls out a bag of mini-marshmallows from the pantry and checks his watch. Outside, the boys have barely spoken a word and are in the midst of working industriously; the day's hard work has suddenly caught up to them and they are indeed tired. However, they have not complained or even contemplated giving up. Out of nowhere, Cruz asks if anyone knows what the mile-high club is. This is something some of the students were talking about during recess at school this week.

Drew-*Yea, I know, that's what my brothers are in. They start smoking that weed, and they're a mile high, boy.*

Gabe-*No, you fool, it's when you get freaky while up in a plane, right?* He looks at Cruz to see if that was correct, who nods his head.

Alby-*Oh, so you wanna join that club with Wanda, huh?* He looks at Gabe for a response.

Gabe-*Why not.* He pats himself on the shoulder.

Alby-*Well, I hate to break it to you, bro, but Wanda is so big, you're gonna have to join the mile-wide club first!* Everyone busts out laughing and Gabe, usually quick on the comebacks, is caught with his guard down. He scoops up a handful of snow and throws it at Alby. Shelly retaliates for his brother and throws a snowball at Gabe. This leads to another all out snowball fight as the group lets off some much needed steam. Mr. Hokato opens the door with a tray of mugs filled with hot chocolate and marshmallows. He watches the boys with fondness as he begins nostalgically recalling when he and his friends did the same things in his childhood. That was before he ever had a single panic attack. It wasn't until he hit his late twenties that he noticed a swarm of anxiety and panic in his life. He has been on all sorts of medicine, but has never attended any form of therapy for his disorder; he remains too scared to leave the house, too scared to feel his lungs fill up with everything but air, too scared to reach out for change. He places the tray on a bench on the stoop and places the cake next to it. He has to hip-check Cash who has jumped up on him in an attempt to get a piece of the cake for himself. Rather than interrupt their play time, he simply closes the door and watches from inside, where it is warm, safe, and far from any panic related trigger.

Lupe Fiasco- "Go Go Gadget Flow" (Instrumental)

After a while, someone looks to the stoop and notices the cake and hot chocolate. They wave to the generous host from their work stations. Mr. Hokato, watching from the window, receives their thanks and waves back. The aforementioned Mr. Hokato was born in Samoa and moved to the states as a child. At first, he lived in California, and then moved to Montana. He became a citizen and enlisted in the army; he is a veteran of the gulf war and suffers from Post Traumatic Stress Disorder. He is haunted by suicidal ideations, nightmares, and headaches. After the war, the Veterans hospital did very little to nothing to alleviate his symptoms. His sister fought diligently with the Veterans Administration; however, there were so many men and women with issues, they just got lost in the system. Now, rather than search out solutions to the PTSD, he just stays home and suffers with it in silence. Now living in New York, he still calls Montana his home. Both of his parents are deceased. After his service in the war, he did not want to be alone, so he came to live closer to his sister. That is also when he found his only friend, his huge dog named Cash, who is his constant companion.

Cruz-*Wow, Entenmann's, this is the shit right here!* He grabs a piece with his gloves still on and eats it slowly, enjoying every bite. Cash looks out the window and his mouth waters as he sees Cruz putting the cake to his mouth.

Diego-*My Grandma always gets this type…and the lemon cake, too.* Cash sees Diego drop a small piece on the floor and makes a mental note to remember where it has fallen. He smacks his lips with his tongue.

Alby-*Yea, but that's from the day old store, this jammy is fresh. We get them cakes from the day old store too, sometimes the expiration date has already passed, but it's still good to me, especially when you heat it up for a few.* Alby can ramble on for days, especially when he is talking about sweets. He glances at his brother who is consumed with focus; no ADD currently taking hold there that's for sure.

Gabe-*Oh, fool, you eat anything, you don't care.* With crumbs hanging off his upper lip, Gabe watches the platter transform from a full plate of delectable treats, to an almost empty dish of specs in the matter of seconds. As the cake disappears like a dead corpse in a river of piranhas, Gabe secretly wishes he had another piece. Nobody notices, however, the beautiful ceramic plate that was hand-crafted many years earlier by Mr. Hokato's mother. It is blue and brown, with a mustard color circle in the middle. She passed many years ago, and it is one of the very few things that remain honoring her presence on this earth. She was the one constant in her son's life; she never quit on him. He used to get into so much trouble as a youth that she would later joke that she had the bail bondsman's phone number on speed dial. Without her, he has very little to comfort him, except Cash. This has not helped with his disorder in the least.

Alby-*Don't hate!* He licks the icing from between his fingers and flashes a big smile. *The only cake you've been getting is from your sister's easy bake oven, so you should stop talking.* Gabe stops in mid-chew and looks at Alby who is sipping on his hot chocolate with such pride. Gabe just shakes his head and whispers something to himself.

The group, now reenergized, gets back to work and is finished in no time flat. Once they have completed, they wait on the stoop for Mr. Hokato who opens the door halfway, which is something of a risk for him. He pays the boys, giving them each a few dollars tip. He thanks them and they agree that from now on, they will be his official shovelers for any upcoming snowstorm. Walking down the stoop, Shelly turns around and waves one last time before the front door is securely shut, and Mr. Hokato is out of sight. Once inside, he relaxes on his favorite chair in the corner of the living room. His sister jokingly calls it the *Hot Seat* because he is always in it; he eats in it, sleeps in it and rarely leaves it. He places a fresh pie that he has been longing for all day in his lap as he glances to Cash's chew toy on the floor, a tugboat that is soaked with Cash's saliva; he has forgotten the plate or fork but decides he really doesn't need those things. The cake serving knife will do just fine. While he digs right in, he notices the carpet in front of the chair is full of Cash's hair and needs a good washing.

Walking down the street, the boys discuss what a nice group of people they have met during the course of their day away from the usual suspects. Cash stands on his hind legs and peers out the window. He is very overprotective of his owner and watches the boys every second until they leave his sight. Shelly sees Cash and gets excited, telling Alby that they are being watched. Cash whimpers and wants to go outside. From the hot seat, Mr. Hokato hears him.

Mr. Hokato-*You wanna go outside, boy? Hmm, me too.* He empathizes with Cash, gets up and walks to the back door. Cash quickly runs to the door with his tail wagging furiously. As Mr. Hokato opens the door leading to the backyard, Cash vaults through the door and runs the perimeter of the yard with his mouth wide open. Mr. Hokato watches with envy as Cash frolics unaffected by the weather or the open spaces. *C'mon boy, it's too cold to be outside too long.* Cash relieves himself in the corner of the yard and sits down nonchalantly. Mr. Hokato whistles and calls for his dog. However, Cash tilts his head to the left and does not budge. *Cash!* Again Cash seems to toy with him and tilts his head the other way barking three times. Obviously, Cash isn't ready to go back inside; it seems as if Cash wants him to come outside and play with him. *Cash?* As Mr. Hokato reluctantly closes the door, he appears hurt and for the moment alone once again.

The Beatnuts – "Look around"

After noticing the sun has almost disappeared behind some trees, Drew checks his watch and determines that it will soon be dark. They agree to do one, maybe two more houses before they head back home. The kids are visibly tired, yet nobody is bemoaning because they are together, earning some honest money and are having fun. At this moment, nobody realizes or can even fathom that this time of their lives is probably going to be the most memorable and influential era of their existence. Right now, they are learning who they are as young adolescents. Times precisely like these are setting the stage for who they will become. In addition, during or after high school, each will gain their own strong sense of identity and will have some serious choices to make. Each will go a different course that may bring them closer together or push them further apart as friends. Furthermore, they each will forge new and different relationships and experiences that will forever affect their outlook of the world. Each one has a look in his eye like he or she knows they are on the threshold of something, yet none of them pursues it any further; rather, they just enjoy the moment. Not until many years from now, will they reflect on these moments, perhaps this day in particular, and realize how precious these moments truly are.

After two more houses, their mission completed, they head for home. One of the guys, Gabe, says he has one stop to make before he goes home and tells the others he will meet them around the block. See, Gabe has not forgotten the old woman to whom he made a promise. He told her before the day was done he would shovel her driveway, and he intends to keep his word. The others give him a hard time telling him that he is a sucker, and he just gives them the finger and walks away. Keeping his word is something his father has beaten into him, not literally. His dad would always tell him a man's word is his bond, never break it.

Alby-*Go bust your ass for five bucks!*

Diego-*See you in a couple hours homey!* They all laugh an exaggerated laugh.

Cruz-*Maybe I'll save you some dinner, if you're home before midnight!* Gabe ignores the hollering from the cheap seats and assures himself that he is doing the right thing. As he attempts to remember the best way to get to the lady's house he notices that it will be dark within thirty minutes. Once he is alone, he takes a seat on the curb and puts his head in his hands. Smelling the clean air, he rests up for a few moments while he enjoys his solitude. Alone with his thoughts is when Gabe is at his best. As he reflects on his day, and the day before, he stares at a car passing by that has just put on its headlights. Gabe gets up, stretches and begins his trek alone; this is his walkabout. He really doesn't want to be returning to the projects too late all by himself so he picks up the pace. Another right, past the house with the brick mailbox, past the Chinese restaurant, left at the corner and it should be there at the next left turn. Gabe gets turned around for a second and scratches his head. He backtracks and makes another left, still not it. As he looks to the ground, he thinks long and hard and remembers that rusty fire hydrant about a block back. He knows he is close when he sees that hydrant. As he stops for a moment to catch his breath, he can't believe that his boys left him stranded like this; but it isn't really their battle, is it. He knows the lady reminds him of his mother and perhaps he is going out of his way to show his mother that he is not a bum and never will be. His mind is consumed with nostalgia for his mother when he turns the corner. He repositions his shovel from his right shoulder to his left. As he scans the street and finds the house, he notices some other kids are already there shoveling the driveway. Walking closer, he sees it is Cruz, Diego, Drew, Alby and Shelly. He stops dead in his tracks and is certainly shocked and confused. Diego smiles as Gabe approaches and extends his hand for a dap.

Diego-*You should know we would never leave you fool!*

Alby-*Well, you gonna help or what, my feet are frozen.* Gabe says nothing and attacks the snow with his shovel, smiling on the inside. Gabe looks at each one without turning his head and whispers rather loudly.

Gabe-*Assholes!* He scans the area once again. *Where's Brixx?* They explain she had to go to the bathroom bad and is going to meet up here in a minute. Together they all share a loud, hearty laugh at Gabe's expense. He does not mind in the least. Alby uses this opportunity to break out some new jokes, since Brixx has not yet arrived. He figures he is still the champ. To be the champ you first have to beat the champ.

Alby-*Hey Gabe, your house is so dirty, the cleanest room in your house is the fire escape!* Gabe laughs it up while Diego and Cruz get a kick out of that joke. Gabe doesn't seem bothered at all and doesn't even attempt a comeback. However, he does respond.

Gabe-*That's a good one. Too bad you wasted it on me. You shoulda saved that one for Brixx cuz she is handling your pasty ass today!* Drew busts out laughing and the others join in. Alby thinks perhaps he was right and kicks himself for not saving that for his nemesis; the look on his face is something you can't put a price tag on.

Raekwon featuring Ghostface Killah- "Rainy Dayz"

Brixx did have to use the bathroom; however, she had another deed to complete as well. She remembered that the house with the snowman was just a few blocks from where the guys are meeting up. When she finds the house where that lucky little girl was making a snowman with her father, she approaches slowly, like a kitten stalking a ball of yarn, and stops in her tracks about ten feet from the aforementioned snowman. Suddenly she notices the detail they added in the face, with dimples, a chin, and eyebrows; she scolds herself for what she was thinking. That little girl worked hard on this, she did nothing wrong. Her father is not Brixx's father; he is doing the right thing. Why punish them? Quickly she notices a tear rolling down her face and wipes it away with lightning speed. From the sidewalk, she can see inside the home; it is well lit and has many photos on the wall. Ensuring she is not noticed, she takes a few careful paces forward. Someone passes the window and is carrying a mug. She notices that person blowing on the beverage to cool it off, when another person comes from behind and grabs them and begins to hug them. There is a lot of love in that home; that much is obvious. Every house is not like hers.

Brixx slowly turns and is ready to leave. She hesitates for a moment and takes a deep breath. As she scrutinizes her shadow on the ground, she notices the shape of it and how it shifts in conjunction with her movements. Then abruptly with one meticulous swift swoop, she swings her shovel airborne. Looking like a samurai warrior in battle, Brixx decapitates the unsuspecting snowman with one blow. The sound of the shovel whistles through the air and vibrates in her eardrums. Her eyes bulge as a vein by her temple protrudes with great intensity. The force of the shovel vibrates in her hand and causes a jolt through her entire body leaving her with just a little bit of temporary pain. She strikes with such force that it seems like time has frozen and gravity no longer makes sense. Mr. Snowman's head tilts to the west as his smile begins rotating until it is upside down. The head twists in the air until it disappears in the icy snow on the ground. The smile that disappeared on Mr. Snowman's face has now appeared on Brixx's, as she admires her work and her swing. Her grip on the shovel is so tight that it hurts her hands and the blood is rushing out of them. Suddenly, the porch light comes on and instinctively, Brixx hauls ass. The entire time, she has a huge smile on her face as she runs down the street.

<u>Brixx</u>-*Told you this wasn't over Snowman!!*

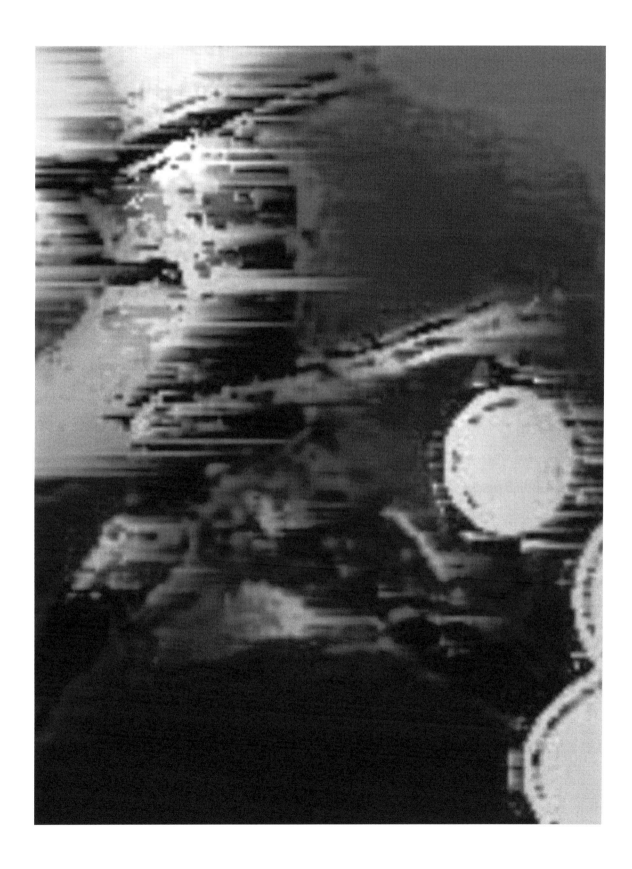

From around the corner, Brixx comes running like an Olympic sprinter. The others do not notice the monstrous grin on her face or ask her what she has been up to. This will go down as one of Brixx's little secrets. She rubs her hands together to loosen them up a bit. Remorse doesn't even cross her mind as she helps Shelly with the stoop. Shelly and her share a smile even though they are both smiling at two entirely different things. Within ten more minutes, the crew is through and prepares to make their exit. At this point, the old lady comes out and has five single dollar bills; however, Gabe and the others refuse to take her money. With an offended look on his face, Gabe pushes her hand away gently.

Drew-*It's on the house.*

Gabe-Don't worry about it. The woman looks around to all the faces of the children before her and she notices such genuine smiles. She wonders aloud how they have gotten instilled with such integrity and generosity.

Woman-*Well, I must say, whoever raised you children has done a wonderful job, and you be sure to tell them, won't you. What a bunch of gentlemen you are, thank you boys.* She smiles and gives them each a hug. It is dark out and she doesn't notice that Brixx is a girl and Brixx is in no state of mind to correct her. When Gabe hugs the old woman, he towers over her and then feels the warmth of her embrace and immediately reverts to his childhood; he remembers what it felt like to hug his own mother. Without the others noticing, he wipes a tear from his cheek with his glove, and lets her go. If he was there by himself, he would probably have held on for another hour and would have cried like a baby; however, in front of the guys he can't be that vulnerable. They all say goodbye to the woman as they walk in unison to the subway station. Alby makes fun of Brixx because the old woman called them all gentlemen and didn't notice she was a girl. She tackles him in the snow and puts a handful of snow in his face.

Cruz-*Pile on!* Shelly jumps on Brixx, then Diego jumps on top of Shelly. Gabe and Diego follow suit and it becomes a huge pile on. The laughter is so boisterous that neighbors come to the windows to look outside at the bedlam. Alby is on the bottom of the pile and is taking the brunt of everyone's weight. Brixx is laughing so hard at both Alby being on the bottom of the pile and the thought of the headless snowman she had promised herself she would deal with. The decibels of laughter drown out Alby's cries all together

Alby-*I can't breathe…*

People Under the Stairs- "Schooled in the Trade"

They walk practically the entire way to the subway station in silence, each one processing the day, going over their highlights privately in their domes. Once they are on the train, they relax and realize how tired they are, slumping in their seats. The train goes through a tunnel and the lights briefly go out. Shelly leans on Alby's shoulder and is out; within seconds he is asleep and snoring. Alby tries not to budge to allow his bone-weary brother to get some much earned rest. During this moment, the boys close their eyes and each one simultaneously thinks of their home, their family, and the families they came across today. None of them could see through the houses like they were translucent. They were unable to see directly into the souls of its occupants to understand the family dynamics. Therefore, they are still full of envy for the way they live and the things they have. If they only truly knew the wickedness, debauchery, dysfunction and depravity that was going on in some of the homes they stood directly outside of today, they would be flabbergasted. Unbeknownst to them, the cast of characters are something straight out of a science fiction novel.

Brixx thinks about Mrs. Eastman and Mrs. Henshaw, then thinks about her own dear mother. People always think it is sad that her mother is losing her sight, but she thinks it is much more unfortunate what Mrs. Henshaw and Mrs. Eastman are going through respectively. At least her mother is well adjusted and positive. Those ladies are dealing with some serious issues; she doesn't know exactly what those issues are but she sure wouldn't want to trade places with either of them. Brixx is the only one who is contemplating this at the moment, as the others are infatuated by the things these people had and the group does not. Besides, Brixx knows her mother has her, someone to help her and appreciate her. What do these people have? Who do they have? She wonders to herself quietly while the train shudders and oscillates seemingly to a specific melody.

As soon as the lights swiftly return, they all begin to discuss the large houses, fancy cars and beautiful things they imagine were inside of them. All of them are stuffed with envy, with the exception of Brixx who has seen beyond some of the material belongings. At the next stop, most people get off and the subway car is almost completely barren, except for the group and one old lady who apparently just came from food shopping. She is carrying two large brown paper bags with a loaf of bread sticking out of the top of one of the bags. Gabe smiles at the lady and offers her a hand with the bags when she gets up; she quickly declines his offer. He yawns and stretches across the plastic seat. Making sure nobody is looking, Gabe takes out all of the money and they divide it up evenly among the group. Shelly wakes up and stretches his arms high over his head. For a moment, he had forgotten where he was. He scans the train and it all registers internally. Each member of the group will proudly walk in their home with an extra 92 dollars, Shelly with half, 46 since he did less. This is after expenses as well: lunch, train fare, snacks. In actuality, they each pulled down over 100 dollars; not bad for a day's work, tax free. Nonetheless, they are all proud of their escapades, especially Shelly who has never held that much money before. He reminds them that he still has the change in his pocket and wants to split that up as well. They reassure him that it is his money to keep. As a safe measure, Alby will hold onto it until they get home and give it to their parents to hold for him.

The train comes to a halt and they disembark for the final leg of their journey. They now walk the familiar streets that take them home. On the way, they begin to snap (joke) on each other. Some may think this is cruel; however, it is a form of recreation for the guys; they didn't start it, it has been around for generations. Alby is the king of the neighborhood with his snaps, and he takes on all comers. He points a finger at Brixx. Before today he was thinking she was an easy target. However, right now he is not so sure. Still and all, he is feeling rather confident and fires away. He recalls she had some good comebacks earlier in the day but how would she react after such a busy day; certainly, she must be tired by now.

<u>Alby</u>-*Your family is so poor, when you play monopoly, you use the little iron to iron your clothes while you play!* He pats his chest knowing that was funny while the others laugh. Brixx chuckles too, but fires back without a moment's hesitation.

<u>Brixx</u>-*Oh yea, well your family is so poor, crackheads break in your house and **leave** you guys money.* The laughter grows even louder as Alby sees he has some serious competition. He raises his eyebrow and thinks real hard for something damaging.

<u>Alby</u>-*Your mom is so fat, she needs a shoe horn to fit in the bathtub!* Gabe and Diego bump fists as acknowledgement that Alby's joke was on point.

<u>Brixx</u>-*Your mom's so stupid she was trying to get a new cell phone and thought taco bell was a phone company!* Even Alby laughs at that one as he now has to reach deep in his bag of tricks. Shelly seeing his brother appears to be out of ammunition, helps him stall and enters the arena with a mama joke of his own. He clears his throat, concentrates on his words as not to stutter, and gives it his best effort.

Shelly-*Your mama so poor, she goes to the Red Cross to give blood just to get the cookie!* He ends it emphatically. Everyone laughs and looks at Shelly in amazement, especially his big brother. Alby puts his arm around Shelly and proudly pulls him close. Shelly feels like he belongs and on the same level for once. He gives his big brother the look and knows he has one additional good joke in him. Alby would never admit it, but he doesn't know if he can really follow that one, but he gives it a shot.

Alby-*Your moms so stupid, she tried to put her M&M's in alphabetical order.* Drew and Cruz give a dap now for that one. Brixx does not pause and fires back without flinching.

Brixx-*Your moms so poor, she goes to the park dressed as a pigeon just so people will feed her!* In unison, all the guys laugh and wait for Alby to retaliate; he is never at a loss for words, especially jokes. He opens his mouth and pauses, he is empty. Even he can not believe it. He's out. He's out of bullets. For the first time in a long time, he is speechless. The look on his face is a mix of bemusement and consternation. Brixx walks to him, and with the back of her hand smacks him in the chest, then passes him by without looking back brushing off some imaginary dust off of her left shoulder. *You'll come up with something by tomorrow, kid.* One by one, the guys walk past him laughing as Alby is in disbelief, a beaten man. Now that a moment has passed, he thinks of one, but knows it is just too late to sling one now, the guys would just bust on him more. He thinks to himself. *Your momma so poor, she brushes her teeth and doesn't rinse, she just swallows, and calls it breakfast! Man, that's a good one.* He smirks and puts a mental reminder to start off with that one, the next time there is a battle of wits. He just wished he had thought of it a little earlier. Nonetheless, he shakes his head and stares at Brixx. *I got one for ya, don't you worry.*

DJ Qbert- "Electric Scratch Dome"

Bright lights smack the group in the face like one of The Three Stooges, as they turn the corner. It is the OTB (Off Track Betting) joint. Anyone over 18 years of age can place a bet on any horse race currently going on anywhere in the country. All the races are sanctioned and carried on television monitors. The guys have been in there so many times and have placed bets before. They just ask someone to place a wager for them and hope for the best, since they are not of age. They all seem to have the same thought in mind.

<u>Cruz</u>-*Ooh, we should go to OTB and place a bet...Wager is another word for bet.* He realizes he just said that aloud as he looks to the ground. Drew begins to blink uncontrollably and wonders why it is happening now. He gets a grip on it by closing his eyes and taking a deep breath. As he opens them slowly, he glances around to see if anyone was watching. Everyone is pondering aloud either to go into OTB or not. Gabe feels they did positive things all day long and encourages the others to join in for a bet, but only if they want to.

Brixx is in agreement and has always wanted to be an equestrian; her father used to take her to the racetrack, Belmont and Aqueduct, a few years ago. At the track, they would first go to the stables and look at the horses, then gage who would be the fastest among them. She recalls how they would study the muscles on the horses' thighs and calves. She can't remember them ever winning though. However, the experience was therapeutic, just spending time with her father. They would enjoy a nice spring day, have some hot dogs, and watch all the degenerates who were there each and every day just like pigeons at the park.

Diego opens the door and holds it for the others in a chivalrous manner.

<u>Brixx</u>-*Thank you sir...*She smiles as she enters. This is her first time in OTB, even though her father was a frequent client, unbeknownst to her. Shelly picks up a racing form on the floor and Alby snatches it out of his hand.

<u>Shelly</u>-*Hey! I found it Alby!* He looks shocked and sad at the same time. Alby reassures him he can pick the name of a horse for them to bet on, if the others agree to it. Immediately, that changes his mood. They all huddle in the corner and look at the racing form. Diego looks to the screen to see what races are coming up and it is going to be the 4th race at Yonkers Racetrack in about 25 minutes. The room is full of cigarette smoke and men cursing under their breath. Drew listens in on a

conversation between two men who are sure the #7 horse is going to win based on empirical data and their many years of wisdom. Drew shares said information with the group and Diego quickly dismisses it, after looking at the racing form. Diego stares the two men up and down and rolls his eyes. To him, they hardly look like they have picked many winners in their time.

Diego-*Shoot, that horse hasn't won a race all year. He's come in second a few times but he stinks! All the races were a mile long; this one is half a mile…he's too slow and would never make it. Bet he finishes last!* Diego seems confident as he glances the room. His grandfather listens to the horses on the radio and has taught Diego quite a bit.

Alby-*Man, look how those two bums are dressed. They ain't picked a winner since they dug deep down in each other's pants!* Cruz looks confused and it takes him a minute to get it before he laughs. He knew there was a joke in there somewhere.

Brixx notices the name of the #7 horse is *Leaving Home Daddy* and instantaneously agrees with Diego; it will not win. Shelly sees the #3 horse on the screen and sees his name, Shelly, flash across the screen. He tells Alby he wants to bet on that one. Alby looks up the name of the colt and it is named, *Shelly Samsquanch.* They wonder amongst themselves what kind of a name is that for a horse. Shelly pleads with Alby that he promised, as Alby looks to the others and agrees that they can bet on that horse. Alby is surprised the entire group agreed as well. He just figured he would place a separate bet for his brother, but this is even better. Shelly is thrilled and stares at the television screen, hoping for another glimpse of his horse.

Gabe looks around and notices all the long-time losers and deadbeats in the place. He promises to himself he is never going to be on this plateau. He thinks they come here and spend all their hard earned money on a race, and ignore their family thinking they are going to strike it rich and put themselves on easy street. However, they are back the very next day with the same promise to themselves. Gabe shakes his head and joins the group in conversation. Of the 12 horses in the race, they all agree the #3 horse, *Shelly Samsqanch,* and the #5 horse, named, *TGIMC,* are the ones they like. They bicker back and forth on which horse they like better, until Cruz has an idea. They can bet a quinella, which means you pick two horses and as long as they finish first and second, no matter the order, you win. Cruz thinks of the winnings then thinks long and hard to come up with another word for winnings. After careful deliberation, he says under his breath, *dividend.* A smile steadily forms on his face like a cloud covering the sun. They talk it over and give Shelly a bunch of credit for picking one of the horses. He jumps up and down and grabs Alby's arm. It is settled. Each member puts two dollars in. Gabe takes the money to the counter to try and place the bet. He feels like he looks 18 to some people. If they turn him down, he will ask someone to place the bet for him. Brixx and Cruz think there is no way that Gabe is going to be able to place the bet, he's just a kid. Diego thinks he will get away with it; he has seen Gabe get away with so many other things. Diego and Cruz make a one dollar bet and shake hands. Alby walks up to Brixx and appears ready for another round. He gets his confidence up and clears his throat. As he walks right up in her personal space, she wipes her hand back and forth and makes a face.

<u>Brixx</u>-*Dam, ever heard of a Tic Tac?* A couple of old men at a nearby table begin to laugh. This is not the way Alby envisioned this happening in his mind. He smiles an uncomfortable grin, while Diego nudges Drew to pay attention.

<u>Alby</u>-*In the morning, you got so much crust in your eye that you could make a pizza with it!* He smiles at himself knowing that was pretty funny, although the delivery was far from perfection. The men looking on laugh at that one as well, as they wait for Brixx's response, if she has one at all.

<u>Brixx</u>-*Oh yea, your parents are so ugly, when they have sex, it looks like two dragons fighting over a rotten piece of broccoli!* The men burst out laughing immediately and bow their hands to Brixx acknowledging that she has indeed won round two.

Eddie Palmieri- "Un Puesto Vacante"

Gabe approaches the counter slowly and smoothly, like a career felon about to rob a bank.

Gabe-*Fourteen bucks on the 3-5 quinella.* He looks the man directly in the eyes. The man has had a long day and quickly assumes that Gabe is 18 without as much as a second glance. The man collects and counts the fourteen single dollar bills, processes the bet, and gives Gabe his ticket. *Thanks man.* Gabe winks at the man and waves his ticket in the air as gratitude. Cruz and Brixx discuss how amazing it was that the guy didn't even ask Gabe for identification. Seeing the ticket, Shelly jumps up and down again in anticipation of the race. Diego walks up to Cruz with his hand out; Cruz pulls out a dollar bill and puts it in Diego's palm as Diego smiles smugly.

Ten minutes to post time and the group is anxious. Drew begins to estimate how much the 3-5 quinella would pay. Each posting is based on a two dollar bet; one could even bet one dollar and win half of the earnings. The guys huddle around Drew anxiously waiting for his conclusion. He asks a man leaning against the front door to borrow his pencil and does some calculations on the racing form. Diego and Gabe roll their eyes and watch a race from California. This race is thoroughbreds, where the jockey rides on the horse. At Yonkers, they are trotters, meaning the jockey rides in a harness behind the horse; it is called harness racing. They both pick a horse for fun and watch the race in excitement. Drew comes up with his mouth open, and Diego puts his hand up to mean give them one minute to watch this race. Drew closes his mouth after Alby asks him if he is trying to catch flies, and patiently waits for the race to conclude. Both their horses lose and now they give Drew their undivided attention. He estimates that if the horses come in first and second, they would share a total of $350 for the fourteen dollar bet. That gets them all just a bit more excited for the race to begin. Alby explains to Shelly how the race works and what colors and numbers belong to their horses so they can clearly follow them.

One minute to go, and the guys all gather in front of a television monitor in the corner. Some old man asks Brixx what horse they are rooting for and she tells him to beat it! Gabe laughs so loud that they almost miss the announcement for the start. Ready, set, go! The gun fires to start the race. The trotters are slower than the thoroughbreds, but can be just as exciting. Alby reminds the group they need the race to finish 3-5 or 5-3 (in first and second place) for them to win any money. The #2 horse takes the pole position and looks strong. Both the #3 and #5 are in the middle of the pack. Shelly asks the guys what is wrong with the horse and Cruz tells him to just watch and be patient. The #2 horse has a strong lead and the #8 and #10 are way behind and no threat. The #7 is in dead last. Halfway through the race and the #3 horse makes its move. It passes three horses and moves into second place, right behind the #2 horse. At this point, the #5 makes its move and climbs all the way behind the #3 horse. The #2 does not want to give up its lead and remains strong.

<u>Diego</u>-*Dam, we need that number two to start slowing down!* He grinds his teeth and looks at the screen like a hungry cat staring at a bird.

<u>Shelly</u>-*Come on Shelly Samsquanch...come on now, please, please, Shelly Samsquanch!!* He jumps up and down and the others follow him doing the same. They round the turn and come into the stretch it is the #2, #3 and #5 all in order. The #3 and #5 catch up to the #2 and they are in a dead heat; all three are neck and neck. As they come to the finish line, it is too close to call...a photo finish. *Did he win?!* They all look around and are unsure. They show the photo at the finish line and still it is unclear. After a few minutes of deliberation, the official results are in; the winner is the #3, second place is the #5 and #2 comes in third. The guys go completely nuts! They are screaming and jumping up and down. The official payment for the quinella is $57; that is for a two dollar bet. Their fourteen dollar bet has netted $399.00 Alby is happy they won, but he can't stop thinking about a good joke to bust on Brixx. He just shakes his head and knows tonight he must go back to the lab and hit the old drawing board.

Rufus featuring Chaka Khan-"You Got the Love"

After much rejoicing, they encourage Gabe to collect their winnings. Gabe goes to the same window where he bought the ticket and flashes his bright, winning smile. Handing the attendant the ticket, he turns around nervously, like he has done something wrong. The tired man behind the counter smirks at the teenager he now knows is not yet 18, and counts out the money. Gabe quickly swallows up the cash from the counter and gives the man a couple bucks tip. He flashes the man a thank you nod, and joins his compadres back in their corner of the room. The #7 finished dead last just like Alby told them. He looks to the old timers who put their money on that horse that should be put out to pasture. Both of them are tearing up their tickets and polluting the floor. Each member of the group will get a quick fifty seven bucks. Then they decide that since Shelly picked the first horse all by himself, he should get a few extra bucks, so they all give him a couple extra dollars. Shelly is beaming and beside himself. His big brother allows him to put it in his pocket and carry it all the way home which gives him such a sense of pride.

<u>Shelly</u>-*Really, Alby?* He wants to make sure it isn't a joke; it wouldn't be the first time he tried to fool his little brother. They reassure him that he earned it and he is ecstatic. He jumps further in the sky than ever before and begins to hug each and every one of the group. *Yay!! We won!* Alby puts his arm around his younger brother and leads him to the front door.

Before they retreat, Gabe reminds everyone to put their money away safely and securely. He scans the room, ensuring nobody is watching them or tries to follow them; if they do, he will be ready for them. Drew and Cruz are high fiving as they exit the OTB, drawing attention that Gabe and Diego hope they don't regret. Cruz looks across the street and says aloud as he multitasks, *superb*, describing this recent event and all the while practicing his vocabulary.

Vinnie Paz- "Keep Movin' On"

They see a familiar face as they enter the projects; it is a young man that nobody knows his real name. They call him Pops. He has a full head of white hair; he went totally grey in high school. The funny thing is, Pops is only 24 years old, that's it. He has people older than him calling him Pops and it drives him crazy. Regardless, Pops is talking to his uncle; the boys have a nickname for him as well, it is Chuck Norris. This man was a very good basketball player back in his day, way before any of the guys knew him. But at his advanced age (he is in his 60's now) he can still hang with the some of the best. Granted, he is a mere shadow of his former self, however, he can and still does ball. Anyway, one day he was playing against a team of young, arrogant guys. One of them stole the ball from him and he and the boy wrestled for the ball. Well, the boy took it from him, not without a fight, and lost his balance and was hunched over facing away from the man. One could see the old man was so frustrated that some young gun ripped the ball from him and he was furious. Back in his youth he would have simply overpowered the kid or outsmarted him. However, on this day, there was simply none of that. As the boy attempted to regain his balance, the old man must have realized that he could not do a thing, and just lost his composure and reacted; he kicked the kid square in the ass! Everyone found it so comical; they lost it and went nuts. The kid didn't find it very funny; he was angry and wanted to fight; the old man was also angry and not backing down. It was quickly broken up, but never ever forgotten. Word quickly spread about the incident. Since then, however, the old man has been dubbed Chuck Norris by the entire neighborhood.

Tripping over some hidden ice, Brixx almost falls down, but catches herself. Gabe reprimands her for being so clumsy. The snow begins to fall harder as Shelly tells Alby he has to go number two very badly. His brother reminds him they are very close to their home so he's got to hold it. Knowing that Brixx put it on him good all day, Alby should leave well enough alone, but apparently he isn't finished, not just yet. He takes a deep breath noticeable to everyone and gives it his best.

<u>Alby</u>-*Hey Brixx, you're so clumsy you need a helmet and knee pads when you take a poop!* That one was unexpected and gives the guys a laugh. Brixx giggles too for a moment and shakes her head up and down acknowledging the impromptu clever joke. At that precise moment, Drew's two brothers race past and Drew asks them

where they are going. They respond that they are going to a cock fight a few blocks away. Before he can ask another question, they are out of sight. *I didn't even know there were cock fights around here.* The others sure seem shocked as well. Without hesitation, Brixx fires one off not missing a beat.

<u>Brixx</u>-*Oh stop playing, you knew there were cock fights close by, after all, that's where your mom goes to get your thanksgiving dinner!* With that one, the guys go crazy and Alby is stunned. They all laugh so loud Alby just grabs Shelly by the hand and leads him home in frustration.

Damien Marley and Nas- "Road to Zion"

It is bitter cold outside and getting even colder, so the group has picked up its pace a bit. Once outside their buildings, they slap hands and say goodbye, knowing they will see each other bright and early tomorrow for school, provided that it does not snow again. If it does, it will be another day full of adventure and making that loot. Alby, Shelly, and Drew go into their building and walk the stairwell to the 12th floor; the elevator is out of order as usual. Shelly races up the stairs with only the bathroom on his mind. Respectively, they take out their keys and say goodbye again. Gabe and Diego walk into their building and stop to talk for a minute. Gabe has a pensive look on his face that goes unnoticed by Diego.

<u>Gabe</u>-*You think we did good today?*

<u>Diego</u>-*Hell yea, we almost made a bill each!* He looks up at Gabe who is shaking his head. *Plus the horses.* He scans around to make sure nobody is listening to how much money they earned today.

<u>Gabe</u>-*No, not with the money, I mean good.* Gabe emphasizes the last word very carefully. Diego seems confused and waits for Gabe to elaborate and he just exhales. It is apparent that Diego and he are not on the same level at the moment so he just lets it go. *Fuggetaboutit. See you tomorrow.*

<u>Diego</u>-*Alright, later.* Gabe could not verbalize what he wanted at that moment; however, he thinks perhaps it is better to just leave it at that. In the end, all that is important is what he thinks, not others. He feels proud of himself, yet he is unsure why. He reaches for his key, and before he puts it into the lock, he hesitates and tries to comprehend this newfound feeling of confidence and pride. His stomach growls and instead of searching for an answer, he turns the key and decides perhaps with a full belly he can find the answers that elude him at the moment.

Ledisi and Boney James - "My Sensitivity (Gets in the Way)"

As soon as he closes the front door, Gabe is hit in the face by the smell of home cooking. His mother used to make the house smell like this. *Could it be. . . no that is out of the question.* He slowly eases into the kitchen to find his two sisters making dinner.

<u>Gabe</u>-*Wow, that really smells good!* They both giggle and smile at him telling him they remember the way their mother used to make mashed potatoes. His father approaches from behind and pats him on the shoulder asking him about his day. He briefly states it was a fun and profitable day. Before he leaves the kitchen, he puts ten dollars in each of his sister's hands, to which they get giddy with excitement.

Drew walks into his apartment to find it nearly empty, except for his mother. His brothers are nowhere to be found and his father has not yet gotten home from work. However, the house smells familiar. His mother is also making dinner and it smells wonderful. He walks in the kitchen, peaks in some pots and in the oven, and nods in approval, a smile appearing on his face. He peels off layer after layer of clothing until he is comfortable and tells his mother that he is going to take a hot shower.

Shelly runs into their apartment as Alby follows not far behind. He immediately runs to the bathroom and slams the door behind him. From the toilet, he screams that there is no way he is eating a dead rooster from a cock fight for Thanksgiving this year! Alby tells his parents about the joke Brixx said and they both laugh heartedly, telling him it looks like he has his hands full with that girl. Once Shelly finishes up in the bathroom, he runs out and jumps into his step-father's lap and tells him story after story about the day out like it was a field trip. Filled with joy, he begs Alby to empty his pockets and show everyone the money they earned during the day. Long before they got into the apartment, Alby had instructed Shelly not to say anything about the OTB and the horses to their mother. Shelly assured him that he would not.

<u>Shelly</u>-*I earned it, right, Alby?* He asks his older brother. He remembers he has the change in his pocket and it excited to show that off as well. His breathing is so heavy his step-father tells him to slow down.

<u>Alby</u>-*Absolutely, you did a good job today. Maybe we'll take you along the next time, too.* With that, Shelly lights up and looks at both his parents with pride. His

mother walks to Alby with a piece of bread smothered in sauce and puts it to his mouth. He devours it looking around for more.

<u>Shelly</u>-*And I picked the winning horse too! There was a horse named after me, and I told the guys...*Alby whips around with his eyes wide open interrupting his younger brother. Shelly immediately stops and tries to cover it up. *I mean...uh...* He is at a loss for words and simply freezes. His mother puts her hand on her hip and stares them both up and down. Alby's glance now falls to the floor, as he tries to exit the room before he really gets it. His mother puts her hand on his shoulder firmly, which tells him all he needs to know and sends the message clearer than any words could ever.

<u>Mom</u>-*Oh, you did, did you? Uh huh, yea, we will talk about that after dinner... now you boys wash up first, then we'll eat dinner, alright?* Shelly tells his mother he just washed his hands but all she does is continue to look at the two of them. They both agree and race to the bathroom. Alby gets there first, closes the door, leaving Shelly on the outside. He whines to his mother that Alby locked him out, which draws chuckles from in the bathroom.

<u>Shelly</u>-He looks confused and asks his mother a question. *Ma, what's a Samsquanch?* She redirects him to get ready for dinner. *I'm not hungry mom.* He looks at Alby who darts his head out of the bathroom and stares him down; he knew feeding his younger brother would blow up in his face. He shakes his head and Shelly gets the message. *I'm a little hungry now...*

Irakere- "Taka Taka-Ta"

Cruz opens his front door expecting to be alone and looking forward to putting a hot dog in a pot of water, or making a peanut butter and jelly sandwich since he is ravished. Instead, he sees his sister; she explains that she got off early from work and figured he might like a hot meal after working so hard outdoors all day long. He grabs the bunch of bills he has in his pocket, and hands it to his sister. She unfolds it meticulously and with wonder, then counts it out loud. Her forehead crinkles into many lines.

Sister-*Whoa, you've been busy? How many houses did you shovel?* She looks on with astonishment.

Cruz-*Who remembers, a lot, I know that.* She takes the money and hands it all back to him in one neat pile.

Sister-*You earned it, you keep it, and you deserve it.* Cruz explains he wants to help out since his sister is doing everything; however, she refuses to accept a dime. He looks at her with dissatisfaction. The main reason he went out shoveling driveways was to help out his sister who he knows is working like a madwoman. He figures after dinner, he will try again and give her the money. If he has to, he figures, he will put it in her purse when she is not looking; that is what she used to do with him when he was much younger. For right now, however, his sister insists they sit down and eat, before the food gets cold.

KD Lang- "Lifted by Love"

As soon as Diego puts the key in the lock, the door opens and his grandfather is right in front of him, hovering over him like a helicopter. Immediately, he helps him off with his winter coat as his grandmother rushes into the hallway with a long list of questions.

Grandmother-*Why have you been out so late, we were worried? What neighborhoods did you go to? You didn't go to any bad barrios did you? Did you eat anything all day? Ya comiste? Were you warm enough? Ay Dios Mio…*Diego looks at his grandfather who gladly comes to his rescue.

Grandfather-*Geez, woman, tranquila, let the boy breathe. I'm sure he is exhausted and would like some dinner.* The look on his face puts her directly into action. With that, she scurries back into the kitchen and begins filling plates with food, still asking a bunch of questions which all go unanswered at the moment. His grandfather gives him a wink and they both sit at the kitchen table. Diego asks about his great-grandfather, of whom his grandfather always has funny stories. His paternal great-grandfather was an alcoholic, but a functional one. He worked seven days a week and never slept later than 6am. Well, one day, he was drunk and looking for two by fours to build something. He bent down to pet a dog, however, there was no dog there; he was imagining it. His grandfather gets up, bends over, and pets an imaginary dog while staggering, imitating his father for Diego, who is in stiches laughing. Grandma hears the laughter from the kitchen and shouts to them both to wash their hands.

Each member of the group is about to have a hot, well balanced meal. None of them are about to feast on steak or lobster, nothing extravagant like that at all. But what they will have will stick to their bones and fill their bellies. The food will be nutritious and not filled with empty calories; it is well balanced and full of vitamins. Even though each boy's family comes from a different background and culture, and the spices, smells and tastes are rather different, one thing is familiar: the feeling. The sentiment is intrinsically the same. It is comfortable, nostalgic, gratifying and something that won't ever go away. At this moment, they are all sharing different meals, but they are all sharing the exact same feeling. This, however, is a feeling that many of the residents in the homes visited today do not have the luxury of owning. Although they have many luxuries, this one is suspiciously absent.

Wyclef Jean- "John 3:16"

Brixx walks up the first flight of stairs then starts to jog, skipping steps, two then three at a time. Once she gets to her floor, she approaches the front door and removes her key from her pocket. Thinking her mother may be asleep, she turns the key counter-clockwise gently as not to make any noise whatsoever. When she pushes the door open inch by inch, she is overtaken by a smell. The aroma of Jerk chicken is unmistakable. She creeps into the kitchen and her mother is sitting at the kitchen table cutting vegetables. Even though her mother's sight has diminished, she knows the apartment and its layout by heart and gets around just fine as long as nothing is rearranged. Moreover, her sense of smell has heightened since her sight has gotten progressively worse, and obviously her cooking skills have not suffered a bit. She has made jerk chicken, rice and peas, and is going to make some okra with squash in a casserole. Brixx questions her mother and she responds that she knew Brixx would be hungry and has been out working furiously; she probably has been working even more relentless than the boys if she knows her daughter like she thinks she does.

Brixx pulls out her money and counts it aloud in front of her mother. Although she can't see it, she can hear how much she has earned today and tells her she wants to hear all about her day. Brixx tells her it was not necessary for her mother to cook this evening, because she was going to order some Chinese takeout. Nonsense, her mother replied, telling her that only home cooking would ease those tired bones that Brixx has dragged back into this apartment this evening. Brixx sits beside her mother and takes her hands. She stares at her mother smiling, as she begins to discuss the details of today's adventures.

Gabe looks out the window, like he is examining his handiwork from miles away. For some reason, he can't stop thinking about that old woman. Not that he is directly thinking about his mother, more so, what she represents to him. His father, who is of the same mindset, looks at his son's reflection in the window and decides to let him stir in his own echoes for a while. He too has been preoccupied by that same woman, his wife, who he hopes is safe and warm on this snowy evening. However, he knows better and chooses to avoid the heartache tonight. Walking beside his son, he rubs his own belly and lets out an ostentatious burp.

   <u>Dad</u>-*I'm real proud of you Gabe. Hard work is something most people are scared of these days, but not you.* Gabe looks to his dad; they are almost the same height. *Some people miss out on opportunities because they are hidden in hard work, which most people are afraid to do.* In another year or two, he will have him beat. *You know I love you, right?* Gabe lingers by the windowsill for a moment longer, then creeps closer and hugs his dad, who usually does not initiate such contact; Gabe has told him time after time that he is too old for that stuff. His dad doesn't bother to question his motives for a hug, and relishes in the affection. Gabe lets go and now has a grin on his face. His father walks to the window and has his own demons to conquer; at this particular moment, he is missing his wife desperately. Walking into the kitchen, Gabe opens the refrigerator and grabs a 64 ounce bottle of soda. He opens the cabinet and reaches for a glass. On second thought, he looks around, makes sure nobody is looking, lets out a small giggle, and chugs directly from the bottle.

Stephanie Mills- "Home"

There is no place like home...
Well, that depends
On your definition of the word "home"

What makes a home?
Depends on whom you ask
For most, it is a place you can unwind
And feel safe
A place that is your sanctuary
Where there are no surprises
Only things that bring you comfort

For others, it is a place where you bury your secrets
Then close the door behind you
And hide yourself
A place that is your dungeon
Where there are no answers
Only things that bring you pain and discomfort
And somehow, in some twisted platform
You learn to derive some sort of comfort from that

From the outside looking in
A lot of places may look like a home
However, what truly defines a home
Is not what it looks like
On the contrary
It is what it *feels* like

A huge house with brand new furniture
And shiny appliances
May never feel like home
And likewise, a shack without water and electricity
And barely enough food to fill your belly
Could feel like a palace
It just depends on who resides in that home
What is taking place
And your point of view

For some, when the word home is spoken
Images of hot food, warm faces, and cool spirits appear front and center
For others, when the word home is whispered
Images of hot tempers, luke-warm attitudes, and cold
personalities dash past violently in their memory

For some, when the word home is spoken
A sense of anticipation arises
Along with a brightening smile
For others, when the word home is whispered
A sense of anxiety and apprehension arises
Along with a more than subtle grimace

What a home should be
Is unfortunately not what everyone has
It should be full...
Full of love, affection, guidance, caring,
Allowing its inhabitants enough room to grow and be independent
But often what they really are are empty...
Empty prisons of pain, shame, and personal humiliation
At the expense of another's selfish gain

So when someone declares they are going home
Look deep in their eyes
And decipher the non-verbal message they are trying so desperately to deliver
Because such a journey should have one of the best destinations at its end
Intertwined with only the grandest feelings in the world
Ahh, going home
Rather than an unknown trek
Filling one with angst and dread
Delivering oneself into a world where damage and despair dominate
To make one feel belittled and small
Worthless and full of self-hatred

How truly unfortunate it is
Some people have gone their entire lives
And have never experienced what it truly means
To go home

Floetry- "If I Was a Bird"

Inside Diego's two bedroom apartment, his grandmother is mixing up the dominos on the kitchen table, as Diego and his grandfather take a seat at the table. Diego bumps his knee on its edge and pays it no attention.

Grandfather-*You're in for it tonight, chico, I feel lucky.* He smiles undauntedly as he looks at Diego and winks at him. His grandmother rolls her eyes and begins to laugh. Full bellies all around as the aroma of dinner still remains in the air. The clacking sound of the dominos comforts Diego and gives him a warm feeling. When his parents were alive, they would all play dominos a few times a week. His grandfather slams down the double six with authority and begins talking a little smack. Within minutes, they are all into the game and preparing their dominos in front of them using both of their hands. Each is keeping a close eye on his or her opposition, because cheating is not out of the question. Diego has caught his grandfather glancing at his dominoes more than once. Looking at his grandparents, Diego smirks and meticulously studies his hand. He is wearing a raggedy pair of socks whose elasticity has been long gone. Upon noticing this, his grandfather makes a joke.

Grandfather-*Better bend over and tie those socks, you don't wanna trip over them.* As Diego bends down to examine his socks, both his grandmother and grandfather are hysterical. His grandfather sneaks a peak at his grandson's dominoes while his grandmother tells on him. Diego laughs along knowing it is all in good fun. Out of nowhere, the thought of going to school has dawned on him. The prospect of perhaps having to face Davis and that dangling half-rotten tooth of his sends a sharp pain to his chest like a paramedic trying to revive a dying patient. Grandpa slams a domino down which brings Diego back to the moment.

In Gabe's apartment, he is on the couch, which incidentally also serves as his bed, and he is drawing. Gabe is a talented artist who does amazing portraits and abstract work. With his sisters watching television, and his father reading the newspaper, Gabe is lost in a world of shadows, angles, and lines. From the best of his recollection, he begins drawing the portrait of the old woman from earlier today. He remembers the lines on her face and the way her lip corkscrewed to the side when she smiled. The gray in her hair is evident in his drawing as he strains to

192

remember the shape of her torso. Drawing strictly from memory, he captures her essence adding her long skirt and oversized earrings. His father passes on his way to the kitchen, sneaks a peak at the portrait, and nods his head in approval.

Dad-*My son has some major skills...I don't know where he gets the talent from...*He talks to himself aloud, reaching in the refrigerator for some juice. Like father like son, he glances around, making sure nobody is watching, and drinks directly from the juice container. After pouring some juice in a small glass, he wipes his mouth on his sleeve and shuts the refrigerator loudly. On his way back to his chair, he places a glass of apple juice on the table within the reach of his son. Gabe continues uninterrupted, and his focus is uncanny, like a small child eating an ice cream cone.

The Roots- "I Remember"

In Alby's apartment, he and Shelly are making home-made sugar cookies with his mother and step-father.

<u>Shelly</u>-*Can I lick the bowl now Mom?* His look is something his mother can't resist as she agrees. Together, working as a team, the ingredients are mixed in a bowl, spooned out on the cookie sheet and placed in the oven. The 20 minutes it is going to take to cook them are going to be so painful and excruciating, that the boys must find something else to occupy their time or else they will go crazy. Shelly shares something that was funny to him earlier today. *There was this lady with peanuts on her neck. . And then her wig almost slid off her head!* Mom's eyes widen as she wonders what kind of adventures the boys had today. She smiles and tells the boys to go into the living room while the cookies bake. Alby sits in front of the television, which has rabbit ears on it, yes, this is pre-cable, or at least it is for them; they can't afford cable or satellite television and make do without just fine. The static on the screen is unbearable, so he asks Shelly to adjust the antennae as he walks by.

<u>Alby</u>-*More to the left.* An evil smirk crosses his face. *Oh, you almost got it…*Shelly fiddles with it with great voracity, looking at his older brother for approval. Alby cocks his head to the side, and an unsatisfactory look glazes over his face. Shelly picks up on the non-verbal and moves it to the left, to the right, up, down, all to no avail. Squeezing between the wall and the back of the television, he grunts from wasted efforts. *Man, you just had it.* Shelly now begins to look annoyed, and it soon turns to disgust. He gives it the old college try one more time until he throws his hands in the air. Twisting and turning, he sees Alby's eyes growing larger. Just then, Alby sits back and shakes his head vigorously. *Nope.* Shelly takes a deep breath and with one final attempt, Alby begins to laugh. Looking at his older, wiser brother with contempt makes Alby laugh even harder. Shelly becomes enraged, stomps his feet, and exits the room. Alby's laughter drowns out the static resonating from the TV until he begins to feel remorse. *Shelly…*He yells from the couch. Shelly waits to hear his name again before he enters the room with one leg in the hallway still. *Let's see if those cookies are almost done.* Instantly, Shelly lights up and quickly forgets the torment his brother is capable of. Once in the kitchen, his mother wraps up the garbage tight, twirls it around a few times and puts a double knot in it. She asks Alby to take the garbage out and he does; Shelly follows his brother closely like a baby

duck following its mother. He walks out into the hallway and sees Mr. Rothman throwing his trash down the incinerator shoot. Trash is placed in this compartment that goes through a shoot all the way to the basement, where the superintendant places the garbage in the incinerator. Mr. Rothman holds the shoot door open for Alby, who gladly slides his generic hefty bag in. As the door closing makes a boom, Alby turns and smiles at his neighbor.

<u>Alby</u>-*Thanks Mr. Mothman!* He chuckles under his breath as he hears his words echoing down the hallway.

<u>Mr. Rothman</u>-*It's Mothman, err, I mean Rothman, not Mothman.* For a moment, even he forgets what the correct pronunciation is. Apparently, Alby has really confused Mr. Rothman lately. He shakes his head and mumbles something even he can't understand under his breath. Shelly follows all the while smiling with only one thing on his mind: cookies.

Nestor Torres- "Besame Mucho"

At Drew's apartment, he gathers all his papers for his oral presentation on *Racism in America in the 21st century*. His parents encourage their sons' education without putting an undue amount of pressure on them. Grades are important, but they are not everything. Drew gets positive reinforcement for his hard work, even when it does not get positive results. Because his brothers are not home at the moment, his parents discuss where they might be, what they might be doing, and who they might be doing it with. Drew knows, deep down, what they are probably up to, but makes sure to keep his mouth closed, like a prison inmate watching someone getting shanked. His parents get settled on the sofa and are ready for Drew to practice his presentation. His eyes are bloodshot red, because he has been rubbing his eyes all day in an attempt to stop them from blinking repeatedly. His mother confronts him on this unapproved method.

<u>Mom</u>-*I see you've been rubbing your eyes again. What have I told you? Rubbing them is not going to stop them from blinking. You've got to focus, baby, it's all in your head. You can control it.* She waits for a response. Instead, he unconsciously puts his hands to his eyes and catches himself. He gives his mother a reassuring look and lowers his hands. In the past, Drew had difficulty with public speaking; he got nervous and self-conscious, however, his parents encouraged him to relax and take his time. As he does, he briefly thinks about how much fun he had today with all of his friends. He does not know this now, but he will cherish these memories one day. Pretty soon, high school will be upon them and they will make new friends. Clicks will form and people will change; it won't be like this forever. Yet and still, these moments are special. Somehow deep inside he has a notion; nonetheless, he could never verbalize it if someone asked him to.

After Cruz and his sister finish their dinner, she wipes off the kitchen table and places the game of Scrabble down. This is something that is not unusual in their home. When she asks him about how he practiced his vocabulary today, he tells her about the assortment of terminology he used and the manner in which he used them. She is very pleased and understands that education is her brother's only way out of the ghetto; speaking with an advanced vocabulary will do nothing but assist him in this goal. Cruz has gotten quite accomplished with his spelling and vocabulary lately, and he has even been able to use them in sentences in his everyday usage. In his hand, he has three of the letter *U* and seems frustrated that it might hold him back tonight. After a few final minutes, an opportunity presents itself when his sister puts down the word, *ally*, leaving him with clear space in front of the word. He scrutinizes and examines his letters and is just about to pass his turn. Finally, after he studies long and hard, he has a brilliant idea. With assurance, he puts down his letters and forms the word, *unusually*, giving him 37 points.

<u>Sister</u>-*Well, well, someone has been doing some thinking today. I'm impressed.* Her eyebrows ascend towards the ceiling as she puts her hand on top of his palm, making him feel warm and loved. Fighting back his grin, he leans back in his chair bursting with pride.

Jedi Mind Tricks- "Design in Malice"

Evening at the Eastman domicile, and everything seems rather tranquil, except in the mind and stomach of the current matriarch. Irritable bowl syndrome has taken control of her colon and intestines ever since the incident on the subway tracks. Her mind races each and every night, like a pack of teenagers with their parents' cars on a Saturday night. Lack of sleep and loss of appetite are common symptoms of depression, however, it is unusual for her. If you knew her before all this happened, you would not believe how far this poor woman has fallen; she was extremely positive and care free. Stress was simply not a part of her vocabulary; it didn't exist at all. Now, it is a recurrent, uninvited companion. She emphatically knows that she will look into that poor woman's eyes yet again this evening at some point. Like every other night, it can't be avoided, just like the toll on the New Jersey Turnpike.

The look of sheer terror in her victim's eyes never dissipates from her memory; it is constant and consistent. She had blue eyes, brown hair, with lines on her forehead that said more about who she was than who she was not. Her choice of lifestyle could be surmised by her clothing. The tweed winter coat was cumbersome, but warm. A plaid scarf lay lazily around neck. The three inch heals were neither stylish nor comfortable, and the traction they provided, or did not provide, were evident. Perhaps she was on a job interview…perhaps she was visiting an estranged sister after years of having little or no contact…perhaps she was volunteering at a domestic violence shelter…perhaps she was going on her first date with a man who had all the potential to be Mr. Right…perhaps…

Eddie Palmieri- "Un Puesto Vacante"

Mr. Eastman climbs into bed and joins his preoccupied wife after brushing and flossing his teeth, which temporarily gives his mind much needed relief. He has been very supportive during this entire ordeal. Not only does he work a full day in Staten Island, but he must be caretaker on the weekends and at night. They have a lovely woman from Trinidad who comes in and helps out during the weekdays. The marriage has had to bear this extra weight, and it is indeed straining like a power lifter nimbly pushing that barbell over his head. After her pillows are fluffed, her hair combed, and her urinal pack thoroughly emptied, she kisses her husband of fourteen years goodnight. He kisses her on the cheek oh so gently. His goatee slightly scratches her face, but she does not react. The look on her face is cold and blank, distant and expressionless; she has returned to the subway tunnel all over again. She can never stay away for very long, like an alcoholic with a bottle of Stolichnaya.

As she prepares herself for another extensive evening of night sweats, tremors, and ultimately a train wreck, she assures her concerned husband that everything is fine; they both know it is a fib. While Mr. Eastman rolls over on his side to get comfortable, she grinds her teeth and clenches the blanket with her fingers with enough force to choke an inmate on death row. She thinks of her painting with the woman being pulled in opposite directions and gradually feels comfort. She hopes and preys that she can dream that dream she had as a child that brought her such joy and serenity. *Please* she whispers under her breath as she pulls the covers close to her face. If she could have that dream just once, she feels she may conquer her battle with insomnia and night terrors. She takes three deep breaths and shuts her eyes extremely tight.

Just like the therapist had suggested, she begins counting sheep. She takes her time, counting slowly, focusing on nothing but her breathing. One by one they jump over the fence. The sheep run in line and jump effortlessly. She begins to relax until one of the flock gets away and in no time flat somehow finds his way to the subway tunnel. The roar of an oncoming train is overpowering as the startled sheep jumps over an oncoming subway train. Once again, despondently, she is right back where she started. Lying in bed, eyes wide open now, she stares motionless at the ceiling. Mr. Eastman is totally exhausted and falls asleep in no time flat. The snoring beside her does not dissuade her in the least. She does not want to go to sleep, can't go to sleep. *That poor woman.* She thinks about her over and over. The window shade has not been drawn and the snowfall can be seen against the murky street lamps. As the snoring grows louder and louder, she tries to concentrate on the snow flurries outside, which has gained momentum, not the woman falling onto the tracks below. The flurries are white, clean, unblemished, with no calling other than to fall…they are falling…falling…falling…

Public Enemy- "B side wins again"

After such a long day, the entire group is utterly exhausted. Bear in mind, tomorrow is a school day, provided it doesn't snow too hard tonight. Preparing for bed, Shelly can barely keep his eyes open. Usually he is a handful to get to sleep, but tonight that won't be an issue. Alby gets under the covers and his mother sits on the edge of his bed, stroking his head. Although he would never admit it to his friends, he enjoys the affection his mother gives him; it makes him feel wanted. They discuss the OTB episode and her rules. She explains how he has to be a role model for his younger brother, even at the expense of his enjoyment with his friends; he has responsibilities. He understands and apologizes, reassuring her that he will do better. She continues to stroke his head and regrettably calls him Allan; he reminds her all over again.

Alby-*Mom, it's Alby from now on.* He sits up in the bed looking serious. The head stroking ceases.

Mom-*I named you Allan…*She sees the disappointment in his face…*but if it means that much to you, fine, goodnight. . Alby.* She shakes her head but understands how her son is empowering himself and she would not dare stand in the way. Hearing all the whispering, Shelly rolls over and rubs his eyes half conscious.

Shelly-*Mom, what's a Samsquanch?* She looks at her sons having no idea what he is talking about; Alby explains it was the name of the winning horse. Shelly continues to ramble inconsequential information. *Why do we have to eat the loser of a cock fight for Thanksgiving, I don't want to…*Before Shelly could get an answer, he is out cold on his pillow as his mother and Alby share a much appreciated laugh.

For Gabe to get to sleep, he has to chase his sisters into their room, since the couch is his bedroom. He is not bitter that they have a traditional bedroom and he does not, on the contrary. Late at night, he has the entire living room all to himself and it is like having his own apartment. Gabe's father walks past with a brown pear in his hand, and says goodnight. Gabe stops him before he gets past him.

Gabe-*Dad?*

Dad-*Yea, son?* He stops in his tracks wiping the pear on his shirt to clean and polish it.

<u>Gabe</u>-*Do you think Mom will ever come back and get off that…stuff?* In mid-sentence he changes the word he was thinking of. The question knocks his father off balance as he stops in mid chew. Before he answers, he thinks about it profoundly wanting to give his son some wisdom. After he takes a bite of the pear and swallows, he is delicate with his words like an experienced mover is with an expensive grandfather clock.

<u>Dad</u>-*To be honest, I really have no idea. I would not want her back around you guys unless that junk was out of her life…for good! That stuff is as serious as cancer; it's nothing to play with! I think it got her so deep, that she'll probably never be the same. I think…*He is now at a loss for words. He misses his wife terribly, however, he knows the woman he fell in love with is most probably gone forever. Sensing his father's uneasiness, Gabe makes him a promise and interrupts.

<u>Gabe</u>-*You know, I'm never gonna do drugs. You don't ever have to worry about that, Dad. I swear that ain't for me…ever!* He looks his Dad square in the eyes, and adamantly pledges these words. *I'm not even gonna hang around anyone who does drugs… for real.* He sits up squarely on the couch. *Only a dam fool would get on that stuff.* He wanted to say, *shit*, but he has too much respect to curse around his father, and his father knows it as well. His father smiles, showing the dimples that Gabe has inherited, and that had the girls lining up for him when he was Gabe's age.

<u>Dad</u>-*You know, that's the best thing I've heard in a long time.* They embrace once again and his father understands that something must have happened to Gabe today. Rather than push his luck, he says no more. *Goodnight, son, see you in the morning.* With his head up and back erect, he leaves his son to his solitude.

Roberta Flack- "In My Life"

At the Gipson residence, Mr. Gipson is busy working on the internet, or so it seems. He is laboring, but only to recruit new victims into his twisted labyrinth. Sitting in his leather chair, he spins back and forth as his anticipation heightens to the point where he considers masturbating. The oven timer temporarily interrupts his plan, so he goes to the kitchen and turns it off. In the background, Donna Summer is singing with her silky smooth voice. When he was a child, and his family took road trips to visit his grandparents, he always wanted to listen to classic rock music. His mother liked opera, his father wanted classical, and his sister wanted to hear disco. The only possible music that they all agreed upon was Donna Summer. He places the casserole dish on the table and allows it to cool off. He thinks about the boys today and how close he was to having his way with Shelly. If only his brother hadn't come back looking for him so soon. Mr. Gipson wonders to himself how many victims he has had thus far in his life. Too many to count at the moment. He begins to think he should learn some slang the kids are using today and wished he paid better attention to the group shoveling his driveway today. If he learns the lingo of today's kids, perhaps his seductions will become even simpler. As Donna Summer sings her ass off, he hums along and prepares a glass of white wine to go along with his tuna casserole.

When he is finished eating, he puts his dishes in the sink, pours himself another glass of dry white wine and heads back to his computer. Within no time at all, he begins chatting online with an eight year old boy, who lives not too far from his home. He engages in extensive small talk until he feels the time is right to imply some sexual innuendos; he is so experienced in this endeavor that he knows when to drop it in the conversation. He discovers the boys favorite treat is marshmallow peeps, and without hesitation grabs the pen from behind his ear and jots it down on a piece of paper, so he doesn't forget to purchase them on his next visit to the supermarket. Just like in school, this student takes notes. The beast is hard at work, ready to destroy the young lives of any innocent child unfortunate enough to fall into his web. With a grandiose smile on his face, he leans back in his chair and takes another sip from his wine glass.

James Brown- "Super Bad"

At the Williams-Lane residence, the house is completely black. Mr. Williams-Lane has not yet returned to the house, after being out all day. His whereabouts, to anyone that knows him in the smallest way, is not a surprise. He is in Staten Island, in an abandoned apartment building, smoking crack and getting wasted beyond recognition. Even he is unsure exactly where he is at this moment. He scans the room and sees nothing but familiar strangers. Each one has a distinct story which is the same old song when it really comes down to it. Zoning out, in his own world, he stares straight ahead unaffected by the foul smells, the site of rats scurrying about, and the unending array of zombies entering and exiting. He has not changed clothes in three days and it smells like it. He is exactly the same as all the other cellar dwellers in this factory of losers, lost in their own consequences of one horrible choice after another. The decisions follow each other like geese floating in a pond; it is so predictable and apparently inevitable.

Using almost all of his strength, he lifts himself up against the wall and attempts to walk. His feet do not cooperate and he falls to the floor, landing on another person's legs; neither of them makes a sound nor seems to care. Crawling like a helpless infant, he gets back to his feet and somehow manages to stumble outside. The light of a nearby check cashing sign blinds him as he leans against a rusty dumpster. The smell at that dumpster is refreshingly better than the aroma inside. He begins to think about his grandfather and the fish that dear man gave him. He always wished he could shrink down and fit in the fish tank and just swim with his fish. He imagines the fish smiling at him and swimming around him in circles. As the fish jump from his hand, he smiles and allows them to be free. They swim around his head and nudge his hat, tilting it to the side. He just stares at the fish as they glide effortlessly without a worry in the world.

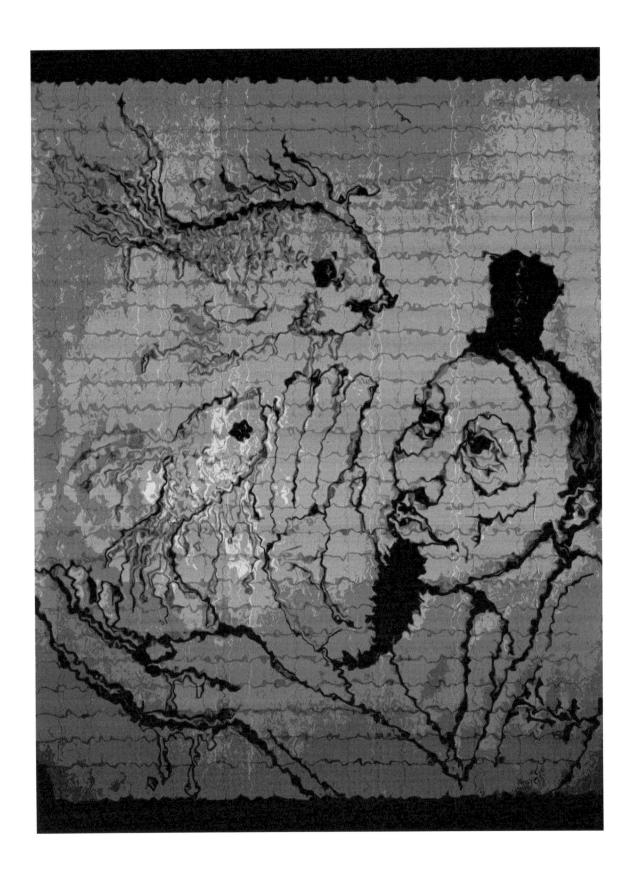

Feeling that his euphoria is on its way down, like a jetliner losing all its engines, he reaches in his front pockets and comes up with a needle, locked and loaded. He slides down against the dumpster, sits down in a puddle, places the needle in his arm and pulls the trigger. Within moments, he is in cardiac arrest, alone, filthy, and with only three dollars and sixty three cents in his pockets. No identification, keys, or personal items on his person; he will not be found tonight.

Ray de la Paz- "Estar Enamorado"

The kid who has everything prepares for bed. The video games go unattended, the many sets of new sneakers are piled up neatly in his closet, and his 128 GB iPad goes unused and gathers dust just like himself. He brushes his teeth, and waits for someone to come tuck him in, read him a bedtime story, or just to give him a kiss and say, *goodnight.* Waiting like someone in line at the department of motor vehicles, he gets frustrated and will continue to wait. He wonders about the boys he saw today who shoveled his driveway. *Does somebody tuck them in? Does somebody read them a story before they go to sleep? Does somebody tell them that they are loved?* As he wonders quietly to himself, both of his eyebrows scramble to the ceiling as he lies on his bed. He assumes they do, and wishes he could have left with them. It doesn't matter where they live, what neighborhood, or the size of their house, or what they have in their closets; it really doesn't matter at all. It doesn't matter if they have a dozen new sneakers in the closet, or the latest electronic games, or the fanciest and most expensive television out on the market. He gladly would give up all his materialistic wealth for one night in a home where he feels loved. As he ponders the lives of those boys, he begins to feel lonelier and clutches his teddy bear. His mother has informed him that he is too old to still have a teddy bear, but he doesn't care. *Teddy bears are for babies*, she would instruct him. He knows that babies have been held and loved. The only reason they give up the teddy bears is because they are emotionally ready to progress to the next stage of development; he is not. He decides that if those boys come back tomorrow, he is going to leave with them. *That's right, I'm gonna run away...that'll show 'em...*Hastily, he jumps up and scurries to his closet. Grabbing a large untouched book bag, which still has the tag on it, he begins throwing items into it without much thought. *Gonna need some pants, and some shirts, and some underwear, yea. . .* He becomes excited at the prospect of starting fresh. With his tongue sticking out of his mouth, he puts his new sneakers by the door so he doesn't forget them, the white ones with the blue stripes which are already laced and tied; all he has to do is slip them on and go. Glancing around the room, giving it the quick once over, he wonders what else he should take.

Cruz is already in his bed, when his sister gently knocks on the door before she enters. They talk for a few minutes and share a couple of laughs. She gently places a cup of water by his bedside, should he be thirsty in the middle of the night. Before she exits, they share a long embrace, comforting him beyond words. Not that this is something out of the ordinary, quite the opposite. He has never lacked for attention or affection since she has assumed the role of caregiver. On this snowy evening, however, it just hits the spot. She kisses him on the forehead, tells him she loves him, as they agree to see each other in the morning. He leans into her like a flower yearning for the rays of the sun. Cruz looks at his knapsack in the corner of the room which is worn and about one week away from falling completely apart. He figures with his money from today, he can afford a new one. Laying his head on the pillow, he thinks of the boy who has everything. He wonders how his knapsack looks and figures he gets a new one every semester at school if he wants. He bets that kid probably has a brand new one in his closet with the tag still on it. It probably just sits there ready to replace the one he currently has when it has finally worn out its welcome. He wonders what school he goes to and how huge and beautiful it must be. He wonders how many pairs of sneakers he has and does he have a pair for every day of the week. With eyes full of envy, he closes them one at a time and swears that kid has to be the luckiest kid in the world.

<u>Cruz</u>-*Man, that kid got it made…*He whispers to himself, warm under the blanket. Stretching his legs out, he turns on his side with a smile on his face. Unbeknownst to him, that kid is thinking about him just as hard. However, for Cruz, running away from home is the furthest thing from his mind. Suddenly, he sits up in his bed and reaches underneath. He begins to bite his lip and stretch real hard. He grabs an envelope and slides it out into plain sight. The night light his sister has bought for him illuminates the room just enough for him to see without the light on. Grabbing the envelope with both hands, he holds it up to his face like a man who is gradually losing his sight. It is the picture he drew for his father that has remained unopened and under his bed for many years now. He blows the dust off the envelope, ensures the seal is still tight, and places it back where it has rested and will continue to rest with an immense amount of care. He puts it to the ground with such delicacy like it is a premature baby coming out of an incubator. After he is sure it is protected and intact, he lets out a sigh and gets comfortable for the remainder of the evening. Stretching under the covers he cracks his back then hopes he can be as lucky as that kid across town one day.

JD Natasha- "Tanto"

There is a continuous ongoing debate that has been argued for years. Does it take a man to raise a boy or can a woman raise a boy and turn him into a man. Most would argue a boy needs a father or father figure and needs a man to teach him to be a man. However, it is obvious that some of the greatest men have been raised by women without their fathers and they have thrived. Some men become angry and hostile, and become the very men their fathers were because they were never present. But others, with the support, love and nurturing of their mothers, or aunts, grandmothers, etc. become independent, empathic, responsible men who can express their feelings appropriately without fear of ridicule. They learn how to be around women and how to treat women with respect. They vow never to be the man their father was, and be better than that so their children don't have to wonder why their fathers left. Cruz is part of that statistic.

His sister has done it all by herself, yet and still, he is not bitter, dysfunctional, or out of control. Quite the opposite; he is thoughtful, strong, intelligent, and caring. His sister has given him the best of her, and instilled in him the qualities she knows will make him a responsible, good hearted man. She knows all too well how many men treat their women, how they take advantage and abuse them. No way in hell will she ever permit Cruz to be that way, and he knows this. They talk long and often about caring. Not just caring about your lady, or your family, but your neighborhood, your environment, your fellow human beings and other things that a boy in adolescence usually has no idea about. She wants him to be sympathetic and empathetic to all people and living things, even the planet. Most importantly, she teaches him to care about himself and love himself. After all, how can he love others if he doesn't love himself. She has taught him to accept himself and love himself. If he does, that love is unwavering and does not vacillate like self-esteem. Self-acceptance will carry him very far in life. The problem with the world today, she told him, is that people simply don't care and there aren't enough people who do care. She encourages him to love openly and give love in order to receive love. This boy will not fall by the wayside like so many others of his generation, she will see to that. She has made him her number one priority and is setting the example that he will follow well into adulthood when he has a family of his own. His worldliness and well roundedness will serve him well as he ventures out on his own in this unforgiving world.

Hi-Tek- "So Tired"

At the Henshaw residence, Beth is asleep once again on the couch. The television is on, stereo blasting, and the lights are on in both the kitchen and living room. The quantity of stimuli being pumped into that house is enough to make a dozen ADHD children go absolutely bonkers. She, of course, is oblivious to it all. Her snoring is at record decibels tonight as she begins to snart (snore and fart concurrently). Very soon, she will be awaken by the smoke alarm that will go off because she is currently baking brownies in the oven and running a bath in the bathroom simultaneously. Multitasking and medications obviously don't mix well; that should be a bumper sticker. Momentarily, she thought about making some brownies for the boys who were shoveling her driveway earlier today, however, didn't get around to completing that task until an hour ago. Outside, the snow continues to fall hard, like a first time skateboarder off of a curb. The streets are seemingly empty, as the temperature dips below 22 degrees. Before long, the snow piles up and sludge begins to accumulate. Should the boys return tomorrow and attempt to persuade Beth to employ them yet again, they will be shit out of luck. The reason being, she will have a very difficult time waking tomorrow, after two more pills were recently washed down with a warm swig of stale beer that has been sitting on the end table for four entire days now.

On the bottom of the television screen, a news bulletin flashes past like a streaker in the park circa 1975. The warning is simple: *Stay indoors because another ten inches of snow is expected over the next twelve hours.* Beth squirms and alters positions on the couch. *Snart!* Both her arm and her neck are briefly numb and stiff respectively, from the position she has been sleeping in. Just like the snow, briefly washing things away and making things seem brand new, Beth secretly wishes a magic blanket would wash over her, cover her completely, allowing her to start anew as well. If only it was that simple, everyone would do it. Since change requires more than a simple storm; it requires hours, days, and weeks of intense, dedicated, introspective work. For precisely that reason, we shouldn't expect any drastic changes in people overnight.

Eric Benet- "Dust in the Wind"

At the Hokato residence, all is relatively quiet. Dozing off in his la-z-boy chair, *the hot seat*, Mr. Hokato appears sound asleep; he has his blanket covering his head and face. All of a sudden, he awakes, arms flailing as he begins shouting something unrecognizable. Another nightmare has invaded his thoughts and it is exhausting. It follows with an anxiety attack, which forces him onto the floor in the fetal position. Cash runs into the room and barks loudly, looking for the root of this outburst. He licks his owner who could use some fresh air. After a few more moments on the hard floor, he gets up and brushes himself off. Walking to the back door, he puts on his heavy bathrobe and slippers and peaks out the window. He grabs the doorknob with a sweaty palm, turns the knob and pauses. After he takes a few seconds to gather himself, he opens the door halfway and breathes in the crispy winter air. Cautiously, he attempts two small steps outside, becomes dizzy, and has trouble breathing. Cash immediately runs out the door and finds a spot to relieve himself, then quickly runs back inside. The panic attack is full blown as he retreats back into the comfort of his own dungeon with his tail between his legs. Once his breathing is under control, he gets a glass of water from the kitchen sink, walks into the living room, and puts the television on. Like the majority of Americans, seeing other people's problems momentarily takes the focus off of his own, as he sips on the water, and scans the room for enemy snipers. The coast appears clear. He places the glass on the end table, yet it is not completely on the surface, and it slides off, crashing to the ground. The noise startles him, as he jumps up, in full combat position. Cash runs around him and barks ferociously. He cups his face with his hands and shrieks out loud; Cash barks providing the background vocals for Mr. Hokato's cries. The night will continue like this, as it usually does every night.

At Drew's house, the lights are turned off and Drew prepares for sleep. The two other beds in the room that belong to his brothers are vacant at the moment. They have not been seen by his parents since the morning. Drew hopes they have not given in to the streets, as he gets his flashlight out and goes over his report one final time. Drew is somewhat of a perfectionist, a type A personality. He is very ambitious, not to mention his own worst enemy. He likes working hard and seeing results. Grades are important to him, but they are not everything; the learning itself is even more vital to him. As he yawns and stretches his arms way over his head, he thinks about school. Momentarily, he thinks of the flattened rat that he put in Lexx's locker and how it must be stinking up the place. He giggles to himself quietly before resuming his work.

At Diego's home, his grandfather places the radio beside his bed and turns the music on softly. Diego has an appreciation for jazz music which he has learned from his grandfather. Currently on the radio is Duke Ellington. His grandparents wish him a goodnight and tell him not to listen to the music too late. This radio belonged to his parents and it is not really the music that soothes him, it is the fact that he feels closer to them with the radio near. In fact, he can't sleep at all without that radio. It is something he is going to have to get over one day, but for this day, the radio reminds him of a time when the whole family was together: A time when his mother and father were alive and providing him with all the basic necessities and luxuries of life, at least to him. His grandmother scolds her husband quietly for spoiling Diego. They whisper in Spanish rapidly.

Grandfather-*Who else do I have to spoil, huh?* He leans his head to the side looking like a curious puppy, searching for a logical response.

Grandmother-*I know, it's just* ...She knows she can't win, so she just stops and smiles.

Grandfather-*Anyway, he'll be asleep in ten minutes and I'll go in there and shut it off...I always do, don't I?* She begrudgingly agrees and they give each other a look like they share a secret. Within moments, Diego drifts off to sleep, exhausted from a busy day. The music in the background is so fitting; it is just like a movie soundtrack.

Willie Bobo- "Timbale Groove"

At the Taylor residence, something has angered Mr. Taylor and as usual he takes it out on the ones closest to him. His son, beaten and with blood running from his nose, escapes to his room and hides in his closet, squeezing behind the shirts and pants hanging in the very back. He sees that a few drops of blood have now stained the white dress shirt directly in front of him and he knows for that he will get yet another beating. He cowers in terror and can barely restrain himself from wetting his pants again; it takes all the strength he can muster. Mrs. Taylor knows the worst is about to come as he strikes her in the chest with a closed fist. Knocking the breath straight out of her, she cannot breathe and feels like her upper body has caved in. She bends over holding her torso for dear life. Cursing up a storm, Mr. Taylor approaches as his wife is gasping for air. He stands over her, shouting and cursing. The son, who is now on the closet floor, gives in and begins to wet his pants; he is terrified, not knowing when the fit is going to end. Mrs. Taylor barely catches her breath and manages to stand up straight using the wall to assist her. Her eyes dilate and she feels the burning sensation in her chest. She is petrified, and runs away from her husband who is telling her to remain still. She opens the front door and runs onto the newly shoveled driveway. He is in hot pursuit and is way too fast for her, but that she already knew; he always catches her. The sky shows its disapproval and continues snowing down its troubled tears. He grabs the back of her ponytail and spins her around until she is facing him, looking up at this six foot four monster.

Not surprising, Mrs. Taylor was an abused child. She grew up in a raggedy trailer park in a small town in West Virginia and her step-father physically abused her, her two brothers, and her skinny dog, Jell-O. She often thought she deserved the beatings but always thought Jell-O was innocent and didn't merit the torment her step-father poured onto them. She stood up to him only when he manhandled the dog, not herself or her brothers. He began grooming her and sexually abused her continuously. He would burn her with cigarettes and throw her in scorching hot baths. So often she thought about packing up her few possessions, grabbing Jello and hauling ass! All those thoughts and plans of absconding never came to fruition, because she never empowered herself; she couldn't muster up the courage. She had a

214

recurring fantasy where she would grab Jell-O and make her way along the railroad tracks to safety, and escape from the shabby trailer park she was tortured in.

Her grandmother warned her that people are like a bunch of crabs in a bucket; when one tries to escape and get to the top, the others just grab it and bring it down. People like to see others' misfortune, her grandmother would tell her, because misery loves company. Grandma always called her granddaughter her little phoenix because she told her she had the power to rise from the ashes of petulance and be something exceptional. Only she had the power to transform herself to a place where the flowers flourish and bloom rather than wilt and ultimately die. From above the clouds and over the mountains, the sun rises every single day. Neither grey skies nor unencumbered horizons could override the blinding power of the light. Mrs. Taylor remembers her grandmother fondly and thinks of those big brown eyes of her dog that always looked at her sadly telling her, *let's blow this Popsicle stand!* She regresses back to that little girl and thinks if she just listened to her grandmother and grabbed her dog and just ran as fast as she could, perhaps she would have the strength and fortitude to take hold of her son now and simply run; together they could rise above this moral turpitude of a life they have been subjected to live. If she gathered up the nerve and resolution as a child perhaps she would have an ounce of courage now as an adult. But now her legs feel just like Jell-O and she cannot move, much less run. Time and time again, she has chosen the obscurity of exploitation over the luminosity of change. She has trained herself to be weak and dependent, subservient and isolated, meek and anemic.

Could her grandmother be correct? Does she have the power to levitate above all this filth and soar high above the soot and grime staring her in the eyeballs? Or will her umbilical cord remain at ground level for Mr. Taylor and anyone like him to just yank her back to reality, back to a world where the evil entities always prevail and cast shadows over the weak and unprotected. She fears the goblins will just ridicule her and overpower her until she is lying on the ground as they dance around her laughing and screeching, whistling and hollering, taunting and gawking. She can visualize hairless demons wearing court jester hats, without any clothes on whatsoever, encircling her while they celebrate; she envisions them stomping on her flowers one by one until there is nothing but weeds and unfertile soil remaining. She was a punching many bag years ago and she remains a pummeling sack, weak and shriveled, worn and bludgeoned, battered and dilapidated, with no resistance, no resilience, and no signs of buoyancy remaining.

Cal Tjader-"Afro Blue"

Craving for touch
Affection of any kind
Unfamiliar with anything healthy
Too familiar with the circles of pain and disappointment
The only touch she had was from a closed hand slapping her face
Pretending it was a gentle stroke caressing her cheek
The only touch she had was by a fiendish relative
Grooming her for his own twisted enjoyment
Betraying her trust
She no longer trusts herself
The only touch she had was by a cigarette butt burning her skin
Burning into her psyche
Scaring deeply
The only warmth she felt was from the ashes
Crumbling to the ground along with her self-worth
The only warmth she felt was from soiled sheets and blankets
Which became her shield of protection
Against constant bickering
And unforgiving caretakers
The only warmth she felt was from scalding hot water
That filled the bathtub
Thrown in and held down against her will
Learning not to scream
Not to cry
Keeping the pain within
A pattern she repeats
Leading to her self-mutilation
And self-destructive habits and choices

That is why she runs
When she sits in front of a warm fire
And basks in the heat
Its mesmerizing glow
Although appealing
It's unfamiliar
Uncomfortable
Terrifying
So she looks for the hot coals
And reaches too close
Time after time
Because of the familiarity
Because it's all she knows

Tito Puente- "Hong Kong Mambo"

At the moment, Mrs. Taylor has multiple and contradictory thoughts. She flashes back to her wedding day; the day she had dreamed about forever, since she was a little maltreated girl. She remembers standing before her husband-to-be in disbelief. She was amazed and shocked that someone like him could love her; he appeared so perfect, gentle, sweet, loving and caring. She was giddy and anxious, as he took her face in his hands and kissed her gently, just like she had been waiting to be kissed. How happy she felt at the wedding reception. He already said, *I do*, and she was not going to let him back out of it. Her dream man had come to her rescue and she was going to live like a fairy tale from now on. Happily ever after as she had read in all of her children's books.

No longer is she a child. Now she has other thoughts: She thinks of hiring someone to dismember him and remove his arms and legs, pull them off one at a time with a rusty hacksaw. She thinks of poisoning him by making him a fatal cocktail with kerosene and rat poison. She thinks of winding up a jack in the box and watching it turn in front of her slowly. She listens to the music and the cranking sound until abruptly the top opens and there is his head on a swivel attached to a large spring. His head now resembles a jackal or a flesh eating demon which startles her and forces her to hide and cower behind an old trunk filled with her childhood memories. She thinks of her wedding album and how it sits proudly on the coffee table in the dining room. What a farce that is! Everyone is jubilant and excited, she was so full of optimism until the first time he struck her when she was three months pregnant. That continued into the second and third trimester. At least she found enough courage to abort their second child without his knowledge or permission. No way was she going to bring anyone else into the equation that she would love and adore, and then be knocked around like the rubber ball in a racquetball tournament. She hates herself and will never forgive herself for allowing her son to be ill-treated. That is precisely why she sticks around and takes it. So her son doesn't have to. This plan, like all the others has backfired in her face literally. Now she attempts to suck up as much punishment as he has to dish out like a biscuit on a plate full of country gravy. She used to dream of Prince Charming, now what she really wishes for is Superman.

Black Coffee- "Superman"

Very soon there will be a fresh sheet of snow covering the driveway, but not just yet. Mrs. Taylor looks into her husband's bloodshot eyes and does not see him at all. When she looked into those eyes many years prior, she thought she saw tenderness and kindness. Was she just fooling herself? Was that man ever really behind those eyes? Or was that just an illusion she forced herself to believe? Rage consumes his gaze as she awaits the inevitable. As he pulls her ponytail and tightens his grip, he cocks back with his other hand and slaps her in the mouth. Blood departs from her upper gums and lands on the fresh fallen snowflakes.

Instructing her to get back inside, she runs with the quickness. Before he follows her in the home, he looks around to see if any of the neighbors were witness to the latest event. When he is satisfied he can continue with the abuse, or discipline as he refers to it, he retreats back inside, slamming the door behind him, and locking it securely. Are the locks meant to keep intruders out or to keep the residents in? On the driveway, the snow continues to fall like powdered sugar on a funnel cake. The blood on the snow in the driveway is vivid and stands out like a purple crocus growing at the city dump. However, the flurries continue and within minutes it conceals the blood, the tears, and the entire driveway.

On Diego's radio, the weather report interrupts the music momentarily, and that brings Diego back to consciousness. For some reason, the man from the painting he saw earlier today is in his thought, yet he knows his fears are irrational and ridiculous. He opens his eyes, looks around the room, under the bed, and up to the ceiling. He smiles and forces himself to change the subject. He now is hoping school will be cancelled again tomorrow, so he shuts his eyes tightly and makes a wish. With eyes closed and fingers crossed, Diego resides under his blanket listening intently. He holds his breath to be able to hear more clearly, not wanting to miss the bulletin. The weatherman discusses things Diego neither comprehends nor cares to hear, such as barometric pressure and a cold front. Waiting impatiently, he finally takes a breath.

Meteorologist-Tonight's forecast is cold folks, very cold; we're going to have an overnight low of 19 degrees and there's a 100% chance of snow flurries turning into a heavy snowstorm. Stay inside folks, don't go out unless you absolutely must. We estimate by 7:00am, there might be as much as 18 inches on the ground folks. . . From under the blanket, Diego lets out a hoot and whispers to himself. *Flurries…*

Murs and 9th Wonder- "Fornever"

At Ms. Henshaw's home, she is done for the night. She is wearing an old sweatshirt; one that should have been thrown away a long time ago. It is old, tattered, and ripped in many places. She has never had the heart to throw it away. However, it is old, comfortable, and has a lot of memories for her. Nevertheless, she lies on her couch after popping a few more pills and washes it down with some unrefrigerated beer. She will lie in that position for the next 13 hours without changing positions even once. Her deafening snoring will bother nobody in particular because the home is not occupied. When she does wake, she will not have breakfast like many others. Instead, she will pop a couple of pain pills and continue with her day the same way she has for many years.

In Brixx's apartment, she is sitting on her mother's bed with a handful of her mother's hair in her diminutive, yet calloused hands. A silver antique brush sits by her side; it probably is not real silver, but it looks priceless. Dinner was absolutely fabulous as the smell still lingers in the air. Afterwards, Brixx took a long, hot shower; she changed her clothes and put on a baggy pair of sweatpants, an oversized Pittsburgh Steelers sweatshirt, and a yellow bandana over her almost dried hair. As she grabs her mother's hairbrush, she sits beside her mother on the bed. Her mother's hair is thick and strong, barely a strand is removed as she glides the brush effortlessly through like a hockey puck gliding across the smooth ice after being cleaned by a Zamboni. She begins to think to herself about her father. She knows her mother does not want to hear his name, so she keeps her thoughts to herself. Nonetheless, she remains pensive as she continues to comb her mother's hair. She could fill a book with the amount of questions she has, not only for her father, but for her mother, and herself as well. Many years from now, she will read the following poem and become deeply affected, wishing she had that kind of relationship with her own father.

Jorge Aragao- "Voce Abusou"

I didn't know it was going to be our last kiss
If I did
What kind of importance might I have placed on it?
The last time I kissed my father, was just like any other
I kissed him a thousand times before
Mostly, we kissed each other on the cheek
As I've gotten older, I attempted to escape from rituals I deemed as childish
However, more recently, we began to kiss on the lips again
As we did when I was a child
Why was that? Was it the plan?
No, I don't think so, it was just organic
Perhaps, one of us, or both of us,
Knew the time between us was limited
On some level, perhaps subconsciously, we realized
That one of those kisses would indeed be the last
Since I was a baby, I never shunned affection from my father
It was never rigid, or faked, always natural
My father loved me, and I loved him
Neither of us was ashamed of it
We didn't care about societal norms or what was expected
An expression of love was all it was
It was simple, sweet, and it made me feel loved
That was its intent I believe
And now it's gone…

I look at pictures of him
Of him and I
And I see the love; I can still feel it
There are pictures in particular
With him kissing me
One of many kisses that we shared
He really did love me, I know that

Even when I disappointed him
Even when I disobeyed him
Even when I didn't listen
And I miss him
I can only hope he knows how much I love him still
And I'm sure he does
I don't think we left anything unsaid
No great mysteries to unravel
It's all rather plain
And as simple as it can be
Broken down to the very least common denominator
Its simply love between a father and his child
Precisely what it should be

Now when I see a father and child share a special moment
I get nostalgic
Unsure if they realize what a special moment it is
Probably not until many years later

Too often there are things that get in the way
And time moves on obscuring your tracks
And often disguising the truth or one's intent
Like snow flurries covering fresh footprints
Then that truth may become distorted or even erased
Making one feel tiny and unwanted
Which could lead to an array of disorders
That was never the case with us
No matter what obstacles stood in the road
He always made me feel like a priority
Like I mattered
And that can never be taken away

So the last kiss
Like so many others
Is easy to remember
Because it was not a facade or empty by any means
It carried the same amount of weight
As each and every one before did

India Irie and Sergio Mendes- "Give Someone Your Love"

Brixx's mother sees her daughter is somewhere else. She interrupts her daughter's train of thought and asks what she is thinking about. Pondering for just a moment, she says she isn't thinking about anything in particular. Her mother then asks her if she has put her dirty clothes in the hamper. Brixx looks down the hall and sees her clothes are right outside the bathroom door. She gets up and walks towards the clothes, scooping them up with one hand and throwing them in the hamper. She stares at her jeans and notices a piece of paper sticking out of the back pocket. When she grabs the drawing from her back pocket, she remembers the day she drew it in science class; she gazes at the sketch of her holding that hand grenade, it causes her to pause. The pin remains in the heavy grenade. She shakes her head up and down and giggles to herself. Suddenly, she thinks about the snowman that she decapitated. She thinks about the little girl, her father, and how happy they must be. Then she begins to think about what she had done and how it may affect that little girl. She knows how it would have affected her. She knows how her father leaving did affect her, and still does pretty much every single day. She takes a deep breath and with conviction rips the drawing in half, then in half again. As she crumples all the pieces together in a ball, she tosses it like she is throwing out a runner at home plate in Yankee Stadium. The ball drifts to the left and falls right into the kitchen garbage as she wipes her hands together three times. From that moment on, she becomes determined to make things right; she does not want to be the reason that little girl becomes sad or cries. Feeling empowered, she walks back to her mother and sits next to her, grabbing the hairbrush off the dresser. She glides the brush through her mother's hair with effortless strokes. As she grabs a handful of hair, she studies the different shades of black in her palm. Her mother senses her silence is more than just the absence of words.

Mother-*Baby, what are you thinking about?* She turns her head around to face her daughter.

Brixx-*Nothing ma… Just thinking…*She blankly stares off into another place entirely.

Mother-She senses the seriousness in her daughter's voice and inquires further. *Well, what are you going to do tomorrow if school is cancelled again?* She tilts her head back as the hairbrush massages her scalp which feels so relaxing.

Brixx-*Hmm…*She thinks long and intensely before she answers definitively with authority…*I think I'm gonna build a snowman.*

The End

Descarga Boricua- "La Rumba esta Buena"

For those of you who may be interested, this is a poem I wrote for my father after he passed away. The previous poem was another I had written shortly after he died. I have written him many over the years while he was alive. These are very personal; however, I would like to share this with all of you that are close to me, and for all of my new friends who by writing this book I have invited into my world.

MY POPS

WHEN I WAS A CHILD
I WOULD RIDE MY BICYCLE WITH TRAINING WHEELS
I WAS SCARED TO TAKE THEM OFF
UNTIL MY FATHER RAN BESIDE ME
I'D LOOK AT MY SIDE AND HE'D BE THERE
MAKING ME FEEL SAFE AND SECURE
ONCE I GLANCED AND HE WAS GONE
I'D BE FULL OF FEAR AND ANXIETY
I'D PANIC THEN FALL
SO WE WOULD TRY AGAIN
I WOULD BE OVERTAKEN BY FEAR
UNTIL HE PUT HIS ARMS AROUND ME
HANDS ON THE HANDLEBAR
HE REASSURED ME THAT HE
WOULD INDEED BE THERE
I FELT SO SAFE
SO SECURE AND CONFIDENT
LIKE I WAS IN A COCOON
NOTHING COULD HARM ME
I WAS INVINCABLE, IMPREGNABLE, BULLETPROOF

WHEN HE THOUGHT I WAS READY
THE TRAINING WHEELS WERE REMOVED
WITH THEM OFF WE'D FLY DOWN THE STREET
TOGETHER
SLOWLY REMOVING HIS HANDS
AND THINKING HE WAS RIGHT THERE
I JOURNEYED LIKE A CHAMPION
UNTIL I NOTICED HE WAS NOT THERE
INSTANTLY I'D BE CONSUMED WITH FEAR
AND FALL

WE'D TRY AGAIN
AGAINST MY BETTER JUDGEMENT
FOR FEAR WAS MY HEAVIEST BURDEN
UNTIL MY DAD'S CONSTANT REASSURANCE
HE'D TELL ME HE'D BE RIGHT THERE
AND I BELIEVED HIM
CONSTANTLY LOOKING TO MY SIDE
HE WAS THERE, JUST LIKE HE TOLD ME
AND I WAS RIDING ALL BY MYSELF
AS LONG AS HE WAS BESIDE ME
HE DIDN'T LIE TO ME, NEVER HAS
ONE OTHER THING THAT HAS BROUGHT
ME CONSTANT COMFORT

I GUESS I ALWAYS WANTED TO HAVE THAT FEELING
BUT THAT WAS SELFISH OF ME
I REALIZE THAT NOW
I WAS TERRIFIED THAT WHEN HE
WAS GONE I'D BE LOST
WITHOUT MY FATHER I'D BE ALONE
SCARED AND TINY
REVERTING BACK TO THAT TIMID
LITTLE BOY ON A BICYCLE
WHO IS DESTINED TO FALL
DESTINED TO FAIL
HE'S ALWAYS MADE ME FEEL BIG,
GRAND, AND IMPORTANT
PERHAPS THAT'S WHY AS A SMALL
MAN I'VE ALWAYS BEEN FULL OF
SELF-CONFIDENCE
EVEN COCKY SOME WOULD SAY

NOW WHO IS GOING TO HELP ME BE STRONG?
BUT HE BUILT ME UP SO OVER THE YEARS
AND I AM STRONG!
NOW WHO IS GOING TO BE MY SOURCE OF WISDOM?
BUT HE DISPENSED ALL OF HIS WISDOM
TO ME OVER THE YEARS
AND I AM WISE!

NOW WHO IS GOING TO HELP ME WHEN I'M LOST?
BUT HE MADE ME SELF-SUFFICIENT
SO I'D NEVER BE LOST!
NOW WHO CAN I APPROACH WHEN I HAVE QUESTIONS?
BUT HE GAVE ME THE TOOLS TO
FIND ALL THE ANSWERS
ALL BY MYSELF!
NOW WHO CAN I TURN TO, TO BELIEVE
IN ME WHEN NOBODY ELSE DOES
BUT HE GAVE ME THE POWER TO BELIEVE IN MYSELF!
ESPECIALLY WHEN NOBODY ELSE DOES

SO NOW, WHEN I JUMP ON MY BICYCLE,
TRAINING WHEELS LONG GONE
I PEDDLE AND RIDE
AND LOOK TO MY SIDE
YET I DON'T SEE MY DAD
NOT THAT I NEED THE ANSWER
TO SOME HUGE QUESTION
AT THE MOMENT, I HAVE NO QUESTIONS I NEED TO ASK
NOT THAT I NEED GUIDANCE FOR
SOME MAJOR DILEMMA
AT THE MOMENT, I HAVE NO ISSUES I NEED TO SOLVE
NOT THAT I NEED SUPPORT FOR
SOME COLOSSOL DECISION
AT THE MOMENT, I HAVE NO CHOICES I NEED TO MAKE
IT IS JUST COMFORTING TO KNOW
NOT IF, BUT WHEN, I DO NEED THOSE ANSWERS
WHEN I DO NEED THAT GUIDANCE AND
WHEN I DO NEED THAT SUPPORT
THAT MY DAD IS THERE.

GRATTITUDE